Golfers at Law

Golfers at Law

THE RULES OF GOLF,
HOW THEY WERE EVOLVED BY PIONEERS,
DEVELOPED BY EVENTS AND
THE HABITS OF GOLFERS,
INFLUENCED BY NATIONAL
AND INTERNATIONAL FORCES,
AND MODIFIED BY OFFICIAL DECISIONS

by Geoffrey Cousins

WITH A FOREWORD BY
JOSEPH C. DEY, JR.
EXECUTIVE DIRECTOR, UNITED STATES GOLF ASSOCIATION

ALFRED A KNOPF   NEW YORK
1959

L. C. Catalog card number: 59–8578

© Geoffrey Cousins, 1958; Alfred A. Knopf, Inc., 1959

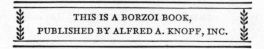

THIS IS A BORZOI BOOK,
PUBLISHED BY ALFRED A. KNOPF, INC.

FIRST AMERICAN EDITION

To my wife

who rules me gently

Foreword

"BY Saturday night the holes seemed as big as wash-tubs." So Mrs. Dorothy Campbell Hurd, a golf champion in several countries, once described to me a feature of the course in the Scottish home town of her girlhood, in the 1890's. The holes had been cut in the putting greens on Monday. After a player holed out he usually plunged his hand into the hole to dig sand from the bottom and sides—sand to form a little mound on which to tee his ball for the next hole. This practice no doubt stemmed from the first rule in the first known written code, drawn in 1744 by the Company of Gentlemen Golfers at Leith, near Edinburgh: "You must tee your ball within a club's length of the hole."

Teeing within a club's length of the hole—just a few feet from the late objective of your putting! It doesn't take a long flight of fancy to visualize the condition of the greens—rough, hacked, dotted with the remains of the little tee mounds of sand.

In contrast, today if the side of the hole is nicked so that the hole diameter exceeds 4¼ inches, or if you find an unrepaired ball mark in your line of putt, or if the turf is pock-marked with yellowing spots, the green committee may be asked for an accounting.

The evolution of golf from a simple pastime to a well-dressed, highly polished, and somewhat complicated exercise is clearly and entertainingly seen in *Golfers at Law*.

But this volume is golf history with a decided difference. It does not tell the story merely of the external features of the game. It is more substantially based. It is an account of the development of the Rules of Golf, and of their meaning; and with the growth of the Rules all else is intertwined.

The Rules, too, evolved. They were not written on Olympus as one all-embracing edict. Rather, they grew out of the realities of play. And grow they did. The first written code in 1744 had 13 Rules, expressed in 339 words; today there are 41 Rules of about 25,000 words, plus such addenda as precise engineer's drawings of how iron club faces may and may not be grooved.

All this might be but a clutter of technicalities if there were no spirit behind it. The spirit of the game shines through every page of *Golfers at Law*, and this is the deeper significance of the book. It is a wonderful spirit which pervades golf, and its atmosphere is quite beguiling: a pleasant and companionable game—a game of fair play, of honor—a game to challenge one's physical skill as well as one's sportsmanship—a game of taking things as they come, and trying to defeat them—a game of Spartan principles —withal, a game of joviality and fun-making. As the author says with a twinkle, "Golfers cannot or will not behave."

Golfers at Law expresses this spirit and traces its path through the years. It cannot fail to leave one with a better understanding of what golf is really all about. In this respect it has particular value for American golfers, many of whom are first-generation players uninitiated into the deeper mysteries of the cult, unlike many of their British counterparts.

Cult? You doubt it? Read this excerpt: "Under the old rules there was a decision in 1912 about a player who started a winter round with a white ball but, overtaken by a snowstorm during the play of a hole, lifted the white ball and replaced it by one painted red. He was disqualified for lifting a ball in play and not penalizing himself two strokes."

A love for the things which golf represents must have been the motive which prompted Mr. Geoffrey Cousins to write *Golfers at Law*. It must have required unusual research. It certainly required unusual background in the history of the game and especially knowledge of the Rules of Golf. Like every other golfer, Mr. Cousins does not agree with every jot and tittle of the law, but any interpolation of his views is so constructive that it is never intrusive. He makes a splendid plea for continued simplification of the Rules and for making them real to the average golfer.

Mr. Cousins is completely qualified to do all this. Although he is a relatively new name to Americans, he has high reputation in Great Britain: he is the London *Star*'s golf expert; he has long been Secretary of the Association of Golf Writers. Even more to the point, he is a player of the game. It is an honor to introduce him.

I only wish he had told us more about Cunobelin and Caractacus. It would be great to read of a match between them and a team of Ben Hogan and Sam Snead. For Cunobelin and Caractacus were . . . well, read for yourself; a local rule keeps me from saying more.

Joseph C. Dey, Jr.
EXECUTIVE DIRECTOR
UNITED STATES GOLF ASSOCIATION

January 26, 1959

Introduction

BEFORE reading very far into this book the reader will, I hope, realize that the history of the Rules of Golf is inextricably bound up with the history of the game itself.

That, at any rate, was my opinion soon after starting serious study of the rules many years ago, and ever since, in my professional and private activities, I have found that rules-conscious golfers derive the most value from the game.

Golf is a pastime of the open air—"a blowing away of mental cobwebs," runs the famous phrase—and in golf there is, or ought to be, no place for the cheat, the ignoramus, or the opportunist where the rules are concerned.

It is impossible to eradicate cheating entirely, and there will always be some golfers eager to profit by the letter of the law to the detriment of the spirit.

But I believe the great majority of golfers are men and women enjoying the game for the game's sake and willing to obey both letter and spirit.

Unfortunately the rules, because they are long and detailed, are not so well known as they should be, and for some years now I have advocated adoption of a policy which would simplify them where possible and achieve a greater degree of rules-consciousness among ordinary golfers. For this reason I welcomed the opportunity to write a book which I think, and hope, will help towards those ends.

Golfers at Law is not a book of the rules—those in force today are obtainable free from club secretaries. Neither is it a book of decisions—they are issued periodically by the Royal and Ancient Golf Club of St. Andrews. But it is a story about the rules (and incidentally about golf) to entertain all players, and, at the same time, a work of reference of value to secretaries, committees, and others who have to administer the rules.

No volume of this kind could be produced without considerable research and the help of friends interested in the subject, and to everyone who has assisted me I offer sincere thanks.

In particular I thank Dr. H. Gardiner-Hill, a former chairman of the Rules of Golf Committee, and Messrs. Cassell Limited, the publishers, for permission to refer to material in his article on the rules in *A History of Golf in Great Britain;* Sir Guy Campbell, Bt., a noted authority on golfing lore, for similar permission with regard to his articles in the same volume; Messrs. Macmillan & Co., Ltd., for permission to quote from *The Story of the R. & A.*, by the late Dr. J. B. Salmond; Brigadier Eric Brickman, D.S.O., Secretary of the Royal and Ancient Golf Club, for his great kindness in allowing an importunate author to study old-time rule-books contained in the R. & A. archives; Mrs. Hilda Kirkwood of St. Andrews for her very kind help and encouragement; and my old friend and colleague Charles Scatchard, collaborator with me in the film *Golf to Rule,* for so kindly and carefully reading the proofs.

For permission to photograph old clubs and balls in the Royal Wimbledon Golf Club museum I am indebted to the Club and to Captain G. N. Openshaw.

No book of this kind can be written without the author's personal opinions becoming obvious. Where these might seem critical of the present rules I hope the members of the Rules of Golf Committee, for whose labours I have the greatest admiration, will not think such criticism unconstructive.

And to the community of golfers, once in the small "cells" of St. Andrews, Leith, and other places in Scotland and now spread over the globe, I make this offering in the hope that it will give pleasure as a story and be not without value as a study.

GEOFFREY COUSINS

Contents

Illustrations

Golfers at Law

CHAPTER I

In the Beginning

IN THE beginning there was golf, but later there were the rules of golf, and then the trouble started. For it is a regrettable fact that although rules are necessary in organized sport, their introduction tends to mar the careless rapture of pastimes unhampered by rigid conditions.

The best games we have played, let's face it, were the highly unorganized games of our youth. There was sport at its best with no rules, except perhaps the unwritten law that the owner of the bat could never be counted out on the first ball.

I cannot tell when the royal and ancient game of golf was marred by the making of rules, because it is extremely difficult, in fact impossible, to discover when the royal and ancient game of golf started. Doubtless it "just growed" and by natural selection has survived as the fittest of the various games, Grecian, Roman, Dutch, Belgian, French, and Tudor English, from which, according to various historians, it has developed.

But since our historians argue without convincing anyone, I propose to let imagination have its fling and suggest that golf had a beginning long before modern civilization, certainly before the Romans introduced to the Ancient Britons the game of paganica, with its leather ball stuffed with feathers.

So I set the genesis of this great game in prehistoric Britain on the rolling Sussex Downs *circa* 200 B.C.

There, in one of several caves set in the hillside, lived an Ancient Briton with sporting proclivities and a wife who did not understand him. One day, walking back from a hunting expedition and followed by his wife, who bore not only the product of the chase in the shape of a bear, but also the product of their marital felicity in the shape of a buxom baby, young Cunobelin spotted a round pebble lying on the short-cropped turf.

He gave the pebble a joyous clip with his knobbly flint-studded club and grinned as he watched it skim over the turf. On coming up to it, he delivered another shrewd blow with similar result. By this time they were near the cave and a third stroke was made, whereupon the pebble, bounding along the grass and then hitting another pebble, jumped into the air and fell into a cauldron which had been left simmering on the oakwood fire.

Cunobelin stared for a moment, then collapsed on the ground, convulsed with mirth. His wife, seeing nothing to laugh at, dumped the dead bear, removed her baby from the sling round her neck, and, plunging two sticks into the cauldron, fished out the pebble.

"That's a nice thing to have in the stew," she exclaimed, eyeing it with disgust. But Cunobelin snatched the pebble, put it in his bearskin belt, and sent her reeling with a cuff.

"Keep dinner hot," he ordered, and, going back across the Downs, dropped the pebble and once more tried to hit it into the cauldron.

Dusk was falling before, weary and disconsolate, he gave up. By that time the stew was burned, and Cunobelin, very naturally, beat his wife, thus emphasizing his masculine superiority and also ridding his golf ego of the cauldron inhibition.

"It is all your fault, woman," he cried between blows. "You took that pebble from the cauldron and bewitched it."

Cunobelin's wife cried herself to sleep and her lord and master drank himself into a stupor with two gallons of mead.

In this way he became the first golfer and his wife the first golf widow.

Present-day golfers will sympathize with Cunobelin as much as their wives will condole with Mrs. C. She very naturally hid her resentment at that pebble which had come between her and what passed in those days for married happiness, and derived what pleasure she could from her children and her household chores.

He, very naturally, began to talk about his exploit and at the next Saturday camp-fire dilated extensively on how he had holed out in the cauldron in three strokes, conveniently forgetting his subsequent failures to repeat the feat. One of his listeners was Caractacus, equally young, equally sporting, and married to an even less understanding wife. The sequel is obvious. Caractacus was up at dawn with his club and a pebble, and inside a week had made enough progress in the art to issue a challenge.

The match was played from the top of Ditchling Beacon to a cauldron sunk in the ground between their two caves. Cunobelin hit the first stroke down the middle and Caractacus followed with one equally good. Cunobelin's next shot, however, was unlucky, for the pebble rolled into a gully, whereas Caractacus was still on the "pretty" in two.

Cunobelin surveyed the gully and scratched his head. Caractacus had a look and stroked his beard.

"I don't see how I can get out of there," said Cunobelin.

"It would be rather difficult," murmured Caractacus.

"Perhaps I could pick out the pebble and place it on the grass?" hazarded Cunobelin.

"Perhaps you couldn't," retorted Caractacus.

"I'll give you one for so doing," offered Cunobelin, but Caractacus had walked out of earshot.

So Cunobelin hacked away four times before getting clear of the gully, and Caractacus, despite duffing his third, holed out in three fewer strokes. But Cunobelin refused to accept the result and appealed to the council of the camp-fire. The elders heard the evidence with becoming gravity and, after consulting among themselves for a time, left the chief to announce the decision.

"We are not well acquainted with these youthful sports and pastimes," he declared, "but, having considered the matter carefully with due regard to what we feel is the strict justice of the case, we rule that the pebble in question must be played as it lies. Caractacus therefore is the winner."

In this way the first rule of golf was formulated by the first decision ever made. Today there are forty-one rules and hundreds of decisions are issued annually, but golfers still argue.

How much they argue is clear from a survey of the literature of golf since the Royal and Ancient Golf Club of St. Andrews, urged into action by a widespread desire for effective leadership, provided in 1882 the first code intended to be observed everywhere the game was played.

It was clear from the events of the first fifteen years of this period that the 1882 rules were not being so observed, and even the formation of the Rules of Golf Committee in 1897, while effectively universalizing the St. Andrews code, still left many opportunities for discussion and dissension as to the precise application of the rules.

Thus, from the very birth of the first code, produced by the Rules of Golf Committee in 1902, the members of the Committee had to give "Decisions." And they and their successors have been giving decisions ever since. In 1902 many golfers who had been brought up in the best traditions of the game were affronted by the necessity for voluminous rules. "Dammit, sir," was their attitude, "can't gentlemen be allowed to play the game without cheating?"

But the game had grown too big and too popular for tradition to be entirely effective. The situation was put very clearly by John L. Low, chief compiler of the 1902 code, himself a traditionalist, yet a man of perception, when he wrote in *The Golfers' Yearbook* of 1905:

At first sight golf would seem to require few laws; the manner of play is simple and there are but two contracting parties. From here to there the ball must go, propelled by the rival forces, the side being victorious which makes the goal in fewer strokes than the enemy; beyond this straightforward declaration of procedure there would appear to be no necessity for law. Nor, indeed, among golfers is there any need for further legislation. A ball lies in soft sand on a portion of the way which is plainly not part of the route proper. To place a club on the ground would probably, but not necessarily, alter for the better the chances of a successful shot; the golfer will in such a case take care that he plays the stroke fairly and does

8

not improve his position. Even when non-golfers had, by a little rule, to be reminded of the danger of accidentally improving the lie, they were not at first forbidden to sole the club, but only warned in a courteous manner of the danger of making a non-golfing shot.

But, alas! into the golfing Eden the taint of Commandment had come. When Paul said: "I had not known sin but for the law" he clearly presented Adam with a very handsome excuse for disobedience. The golfer at once began to wonder why he had been told to guard against unfair work in the bunker, and the non-golfer to apply himself more assiduously to the art of acting within the near letter of the law. But both sections of the golfing world were compelling into being the forensic forces which have since grasped the game with the stern hand of technicality.

The just man played as before, taking no advantage of the law; the unjust grounded his club as freely as he dared. Between these two extremes a game was possible, for the golfer saw nothing of the evil ways of his adversary; he knew sin only by hearsay and had not become intimate with it. But when the wily ones met, the subtlety of sin began to develop and soon became a fair ground of argument.

The refinements of law-breaking became too difficult of distinguishment and once again the law had to make more perfect the knowledge of sin. So it came about that the law decreed that the bunker-entrapped golfer had to quit his troubles with club unsoled—the first of a race who could not be trusted and needed the law to birch-rod them into the ways of honesty.

It would be tedious to toil the gradations which have

led up to the present position of the law. The rules have been altered for the most part in order to meet some special objection or case, and often, as it seems to be, altered for the worse in order to satisfy some local condition.

At present we hear some talk of a simplified code, but the people who are asking for a shorter table of laws are the same who send up their riddles to the Press and to the Rules of Golf Committee, and are indignant if their extraordinary set of circumstances is not fully provided for by the existing code.

Personally, I do not think that under any code there has been any real difficulty in understanding the meaning of the law. And this view is borne out by the fact that, in all the hundreds of matches played in the Amateur Championships and in the big money matches which have been fought out by amateurs and by professionals, there has, so far as I am aware, hardly been a single case in which the rules of the game led to any misunderstanding between the players; I refer of course to matters of law, not matters of fact. And yet the rules have apparently needed constant addition, and constant explanation.

The pity of golf today is that men play entirely to win and are afraid that they may be defrauded by some inequality of penalty from gaining the end of their desire. It would be happier for golf if we would only remember that the true good is in the playing, not in the winning; and that the man who does his best and loses has wrought his part as bravely as the winner and is entitled to feel an equal satisfaction in the day's engagement.

The golfer is nowadays too often trying to escape by

a rule from his present circumstance. He wishes to know if he can lift and lose one or lift and lose two; and if so where he can drop his ball. If only the spirit could come to him which would show him that it is his duty to play on, though his ball is in an evil place, and trust for things to right themselves, the game would be beginning to emerge from the meaner condition into which circumstances have forced it, and gain again its purer and simpler form.

Those words were written just over half a century ago. I quote them now because they might have been written today, and because John Low so admirably expresses my own sentiments. Cunobelin, in my fable, wanted to "lift and lose one"; the elders said he must play the pebble as it lay; and in those days the word of the elders was law.

Today there are far too many Cunobelins and far too few elders combining austerity with authority. But anyone who says so is but a voice crying in the wilderness.

CHAPTER II

Growth of the Rules

THE idea of submitting disputes to a referee, whether a judge, an arbitrator, a council, or a committee, is probably older than civilization, since it was no doubt practised to a limited extent in the animal kingdom before the human race evolved.

But it is a defect of civilization that as a community grows, so the need for legal control increases. The rough-and-ready justice of the chieftain in his hut or the elders at the camp-fire would serve in a small, self-contained community because the disputes could be settled quickly by referees all well acquainted with the individuals concerned and the circumstances of the case.

Growth of a community not only in numbers but in area would inevitably create difficulties in the administration of justice, and virtually impose on the chief the necessity for having more judges and, in the end, some written or traditional guide to the handling of cases.

Since the chief assisted by his wise men could no longer decide every case personally and on his hearth, he would delegate his powers to others acting in his name, and these representative judges would be provided with written or oral instructions based on previous experience.

It is easy to understand how this kind of development occurred in golf.

First there were the golfers of one community, carrying on their matches over ground untrammelled by boundaries and guided by no law save the primary law of the survival of the fittest. Disputes between them could be settled locally either by argument between themselves or by reference to the opinion of comrades who would be able to draw on the experience of previous cases.

There is no doubt that prior to 1744 golf was played mainly on such terms, and the golfers of Edinburgh, like those of other localities in Scotland, would be controlled by tacit agreements rather than by written rules, and in the event of dispute would accept the opinions of the most experienced of their number.

But this system, adequate to deal with the occasional disputes arising from a match between friends, was impracticable and totally inadequate when applied to a competition in which the per-

formances of the whole field, and not the fortunes of
two protagonists, determined the result.

In such cases it would be essential for every
competitor to play under the same conditions, subject, of course, to the vagaries of weather, and it is
to this circumstance that we owe the institution of
the first known code of rules.

Golf had been played in Scotland for many
years, perhaps for several centuries, before the
middle of the eighteenth century provided history
with its first examples of golf clubs, or societies. By
that time Edinburgh must have become a great
center of the game, since there is evidence that not
only kings and nobles but also burgesses and
commoners played golf.

In fact, knowing that in 1681 the Duke of York
(afterwards James II) played in a foursome with
John Paterson, a shoemaker, as his partner, we may
assume that long before the Stuart dynasty united
the crowns of England and Scotland the links at
Leith were the resort of Edinburgh citizens of all
classes for the purpose of "playing at the Goff."

Apart from the historical case already mentioned,
it is probable that in those days the noble and high-
born inhabitants of the Scottish capital kept mostly
to themselves, playing matches over the five holes
of Leith for wagers of claret and port, and repairing
to the house of one of them, or to a respectable
hostelry, to talk over the events of the day and strike
wagers for the games of the morrow.

Those matches would be arranged by mutual agreement as to conditions. One important question would be the handicap, or the odds to be given by the stronger side to the weaker. This would often occasion an argument which could be settled by appeals to other golfers present, or by one side or the other refusing to play the match on the terms suggested. Similar decisions would have to be made about other points of the proposed match, and, while in the earliest days such details would have to be agreed upon for each separate match, in time a practical unwritten code of behaviour would have developed.

Some examples of this in a close community can be observed in most golf clubs today. For instance, at my own golf club one member of a fourball match will suggest playing for "Club Stakes," and the other three agree. Although nothing more is said, all four golfers are aware that the match is for half-a-crown a side, with sixpences for birdies. But such things are dependent on all or most of those concerned "knowing the ropes" and understanding each other's point of view, much as one particular set of schoolboys will have their own particular rules for playing marbles or pitch-and-toss, and those of the next neighbourhood different rules.

In 1744, however, the select circle of respectable Leith golfers formed themselves into what was at first known as the Company of Gentlemen Golfers and is now the Honourable Company of Edinburgh

Golfers. The first President was Duncan Forbes of Culloden, who ranked as one of the foremost golfers of the day, and there is no doubt he had a great deal to do with the decision of the Lord Provost and the City Fathers of Edinburgh to present a silver club for competition on the Leith links.

The club cost fifteen Scots pounds and was to be played for yearly on the first Monday in April by "fit and proper persons" paying five shillings each entry money. According to an account in the *Scots Magazine* of 1744, the winner was to be styled "Captain of the Goff" and in that office "have the sole disposal of the booking money, the determination of disputes among golfers with the assistance of two or three of the players, and the superintendency of the links."

Mr. John Rattray, a surgeon in Edinburgh, won that opening competition for the Silver Club, and so may be regarded as the first Captain of Golf and the first chairman of the first Rules of Golf Committee.

But what we cannot find from history is the exact form of the competition. The *Scots Magazine* extract states that the players were to be matched into

parties of twos, or of threes if their number be great, by lot; that the player who shall have won the greatest number of holes, be victor; and if two or more shall have won an equal number, that they play a round by themselves in order to determine the match.

This famous picture, more than a century old, shows clearly how restricted was the space for putting in those days. The ground outside a radius of two or three yards from the hole is rough and broken. Allowing for the artist's license in arranging his group, the poor man putting is doing so under difficulties. Gambling onlookers, ginger beer on sale, and a most animated conversation all within a few yards from him—no wonder he looks as though he will miss.

The Victorian artist shows a family party, perhaps on the way home from church, watching this strange game of golf on Blackheath. They might wonder, too, at the bandy-legged putting-stance and the curious sledgehammer swing of the golfer in the distance. The surface of the "putting green" would not bear inspection by the golfer of today.

The idea that this was a match-play knock-out tournament cannot be entertained because there was a plan to send out players in threes if the entry were large. It is possible that the ten entrants played five matches and that Mr. Rattray won his match by the greatest margin of "holes up"—the common system of playing matches in those days.

There is no evidence that this first competition was a stroke-play competition; nevertheless we do know it was thrown open to "noblemen, gentlemen and others from the United Kingdom and Ireland" who came forward with five shillings sterling for entry money. And we can imagine the anxiety of the "locals," the members of this new Company of Gentlemen Golfers, to ensure that any golfer coming from other parts of the British Isles should be aware of the customs current on the links of Leith.

In this way the world of golf was blessed with the first written code of rules—or, at any rate, the first written code which has come down to us. It consisted of thirteen rules, and quite clearly was applicable only to match-play, a circumstance which confirms the impression that this first competition for the Silver Club was by some combination of matches.

Under Rule 5 the golfer was told he could re-move his ball from water "or watery filth," tee it behind, and play it, but would have to allow his adversary a stroke "for so getting the ball."

Similarly, under Rule 7 the player is adjured in putting "to play your ball honestly for the hole, and

17

not to play on your adversary's ball, not lying in your way to the hole."

These first rules were, as I have said, only thirteen in number and were commendably brief in substance, but it was not long before they were found to be the object of argument and dispute.

Rule 5, already referred to, seems to be perfectly clear. But Rule 13 in its original form was ambiguous, since, while it stated that works for the preservation of the course, the Scholars' Holes, and the Soldiers' Lines were not hazards, and that the ball was to be taken out from them, teed, and played, it did not state what, if any, the penalty was to be.

So in the first minute book of the Company of Gentlemen Golfers, after the 1744 rules signed by Mr. Rattray, we find over the signature of a later captain the following:

The 5th and 13th articles of the foregoing laws having occasioned frequent disputes it is found convenient that in all time coming the law shall be: That in No Case Whatsoever a ball shall be lifted without losing a stroke except it is in the Scholars' Holes, when it may be taken out, teed, and played with any club without losing a stroke—and in all other cases the ball must be played where it lies except it is at least half-covered with water or filth, when it may if the player chuses, be taken out, teed and played with any club upon loosing [*sic*] a stroke.

No doubt the Committee of the Company of Gentlemen Golfers, assembled under their captain,

Thomas Boswall, and deciding on this momentous revision, were convinced they had settled all such questions for ever. Witness the confident phrase "in all time coming."

Little did they know that their pronouncement was but the first recorded Decision on the Rules of Golf, that for two centuries to come there would be periodical revisions, decisions without end, and still the wrangling and the discussions among golfers on questions of interpretation and application.

Writing in the *Golfing Annual* of 1889-90, a few years after the St. Andrews code of rules was published, a contributor refers to "the anomalies which are unfortunately still to be found in the laws of golf, notwithstanding the many suggestions made in the direction of reform."

He describes the formation of a golf club near London and how some of the members wanted to play St. Andrews rules and others the rules of an older club some miles away.

In the case of a lost ball some players wanted permission to tee another ball, under a penalty of two strokes, as near as possible to where the lost ball was believed to have finished.

The writer in the *Golfing Annual* supported this suggestion, and the more conservative players of the period no doubt hastened to point out that it was bad in law, offending against the principle that the stipulated course must be played. Yet it must be recalled that a rule of this kind was introduced by

19

the Honourable Company in 1775 and was so much in favour with golfers of the time that it lasted, at least in the Edinburgh area, for sixty-four years!

It is a question of fact where the ball was played from, and it is the responsibility of the player to drop another ball "as near as possible" to that spot, and the responsibility of the fellow competitor or marker to see that he does so. On the other hand, it is not a question of fact that because a ball was seen to dive into a particular patch of bushes or rough country, it is resting there. It may have shot forward, jumped back, or hit something hard and bounced out of bounds.

The only fact which the laws will accept is the physical presence of the ball, and it can easily be appreciated that any departure from this funda-mental law could open the door to all kinds of abuses.

But our authority was writing in days long before the provisional ball (see page 78) had been thought of, and he was concerned, as no doubt many of his fellow golfers were, at the congestion and frustration caused by players having to go back to play another ball, the first having been "lost."

Another section of members of the club con-cerned wanted to regard hoof marks in the same light as spots scraped by rabbits and allow a lift from these and other depressions without penalty. It was sug-gested (and was indeed foreshadowing a later rule) that any hole in which the ball was below the level of the ground should be in the category of holes from which free lifts could be made.

Having dealt with these and other contentious points, the writer concludes:

All this will doubtless be considered very heretical and presumptuous by those old players who have been nurtured in the traditions of the ancient game; and the writer formulates these objections with all diffidence and humility. It appears to him, however, that those who have to do with the spread of golf in new neighbourhoods and who are endeavouring to make players of the thousands of busy brain workers to whom this noble pastime is the only one available, should look to the greatest good of the greatest number, rather than to the upholding of ancient custom.

If, as the writer believes, the feeling in favour of a more catholic and comprehensive code of rules is widespread among the multitude of educated and thinking men who have taken up the game during the last year or two a responsibility devolves upon those who are recognized as prominent golfers to make some definite movement with a view to the appointment of a representative body, who shall make an authoritative settlement of the many points on which differences exist.

Well, well. So there were philistines even eighty years ago trying to overturn the ancient moss-grown stones of tradition.

The article quoted above was published about two years after the Royal and Ancient Golf Club of

St. Andrews had produced a "universal" code, and a few months after Royal Blackheath and the Honourable Company had in turn accepted the St. Andrews code.

Yet the confusion and dissension revealed by this article had not suddenly developed, for in 1885 the Royal Wimbledon Club had appealed to the R. & A. to form an association of golf clubs bound to accept a uniform code.

The Royal Wimbledon Club was well qualified to play an important part in such negotiations, having a number of knowledgeable and influential rule-makers, including the honorary secretary, Mr. Henry A. Lamb. The Royal Wimbledon code of 1883, signed by Mr. Lamb, was in some respects in advance of current thought in Scotland. It was the first to make an attempt to incorporate procedure for both match- and medal-play in the same rule, although it did have some special rules for medal-play. It allowed an unplayable ball to be teed behind for two strokes in match-play as well as medal-play; and applied the "stroke and distance" rule to a lost ball in both forms of golf. And it included a rule, subsequently adopted by St. Andrews, that the ball must be fairly struck and not pushed, scraped, or spooned. Royal Wimbledon golfers also, I believe, were the first to define a stroke as "a movement of the club made with the intention of striking at the ball."

When the first St. Andrews attempt at a uni-

versal code was made in 1882, Royal Wimbledon
and some other clubs, including Royal Blackheath
and the Honourable Company, continued to play
under their own rules, a matter for increasing dis-
satisfaction among golfers now circulating among
various golfing centres, and only partially remedied
by the R. & A. code of 1888. This for the first time
separated the Rules of Golf from those rules which
had particular reference to situations which might
arise on the Old Course at St. Andrews, such as a ball
in the Swilcan Burn, the "Station-Master's Garden,"
and the Eden River, or lying near "the seat at the
High Hole." These were incorporated in a section
headed "Local Rules for St. Andrews Links," and now
at last the world of golf had a code which answered
most of the criticisms.

Royal Wimbledon, Royal Blackheath, and the
Honourable Company accepted this code, but apparently not without suggestions for improvement, for
in 1890, following an approach to the R. & A. by
delegates of clubs represented at the Amateur
Championship, a special committee was set up to
revise the rules.

The new code was produced in 1892, but there
was no legislative force behind it and the agitation
for some form of central government of the game
continued.

In 1896 this end was almost achieved, but failed
because the leading English clubs wanted a committee composed half of R. & A. representatives and

half of representatives of other clubs; whereas most of the Scottish clubs wanted the R. & A. to be in supreme control.

This could easily have led to a schism, but the English clubs capitulated after the R. & A. meeting had thrown out the motion and the special committee resigned. In 1897 the proposal was renewed in accordance with the wishes of the Scottish clubs and the first Rules of Golf Committee came into existence.

It consisted of fifteen members of the R. & A. with power to deal with proposals relating to or questions of interpretation arising on the rules and customs of golf. On all such questions it was to be the final authority. On the other hand, it was laid down that any resolution to amend or repeal an existing rule or to make new rule or rules must be endorsed by a two-thirds majority of R. & A. members at a general meeting.

Although these terms of reference have not changed, the Committee now consists of twelve members of the R. & A. and not more than eight representatives of other bodies, invited annually by the twelve elected members. At present these co-opted members consist of one each from South Africa, Australia, Canada, New Zealand, the European Golf Federation, and the British Golf Unions' Joint Advisory Council, and two from the United States.

This development of the Rules of Golf Committee from a body recruited solely from members of one club to an organization incorporating the opinions of the whole world of golf was a natural development, without which the authority of the R. & A. could not have been maintained. Despite this broadening of representation, there have been differences of opinion between the United States Golf Association and the Royal and Ancient Golf Club, and for some years after the war the two countries had separate codes.

But in 1951 efforts to end this schism were stepped up. A representative body of U.S.G.A. delegates came over with the U. S. Walker Cup team of that year and agreement was reached. Once more the whole golf world was united under one code of rules, and it has so remained. There is one trifling exception, for the size of the ball is different under U.S. rules from that of the British ball. But that is merely a question of national preference, based on the different conditions of golf in the respective countries, and does not alter the fact that there is Anglo-American amity on actual conditions of playing the game.

One anachronism persists, for no alteration or introduction of a rule can take place without the approval of two thirds of the members of the R. & A.

In theory this confers the power of veto on ordinary members of a club, none of whom has necessarily any ability or knowledge to judge an issue affecting the playing conditions of millions of golfers. In practice, however, the recommendations of the Rules of Golf Committee are endorsed by the business meetings of the R. & A.

And the present international composition of the Committee ensures that the opinions of Commonwealth, American, and European organizations are voiced when any important matter is deliberated.

It is now necessary to return to the period from 1936 to 1946 to show how British and American ideas first diverged and then came together again.

The 1934 code was formulated by the R. & A. and the U.S.G.A. in consultation, but two years later the first American departure was the introduction of a modified "stymie rule," allowing a ball lying within six inches of the hole to be lifted if it was interfering with the play of an opponent, no matter how great the distance between the two balls. Britain, of course, adhered to the timed-honoured rule permitting this to be done only if the two balls were within six inches of each other, and irrespective of their distance from the hole.

In 1938 a suggestion came from the United States for a simplified code in which, among other improvements, the rules for medal-play and match-play were to be combined. Before Anglo-American discussions could take place, war broke out, and the idea was virtually shelved in this country. But thought had evidently been proceeding along those lines in America, because in 1946, before St. Andrews had had time to return to peaceful contemplation of the state of golf, the U.S.G.A. introduced a unilateral code which not only followed out the idea of combining match- and medal-play and retained the American conception of the "stymie rule," but also reduced the penalty for Out of Bounds to "distance only." This code also contained a long and exhaustive, not to say exhausting, list of "obstructions," and other alleged improvements which provided full evidence that the U.S. rule-makers had allowed enthusiasm to outrun discretion in the provision of something digestible by the golfing public.

Around this time British law-makers were working in various camps on the task of revision and simplification of the 1934 code, and the ultimate result, achieved not without argument and acrimony, was a very much simplified, even a revolutionary, code, which was approved by the R. & A. autumn business meeting in 1949 to be in force for an experimental period of two years.

This code reduced penalties considerably, mainly because it substituted "distance only" for "stroke and distance" in the cases of Lost, Out of Bounds, and Unplayable balls, and as a matter of equity the traditional penalty of two strokes in a competition or loss of hole in a match had in most cases to be reduced to one stroke.

The move towards lighter penalties was begun in 1938 when proposals to that effect were put forward by the late Lieutenant-Colonel M. E. Lindsay. A sub-committee of the Rules of Golf Committee of St. Andrews started to investigate these, but the war suspended the activities. Nevertheless, Colonel Lindsay continued to maintain an interest in the project and exchanged views from 1939 to 1946, while a member of the Rules of Golf Committee, with Mr. James Buchanan, of the Royal Canadian Golf Association. As a result, they jointly submitted to St. Andrews in 1947 "Suggested Amendments to the Rules of Golf," and in introducing them Colonel Lindsay wrote:

Revolutionary changes have been made, especially in the reduction of penalties. As you are doubtless aware there is slowly creeping into the game a contempt for the Rules of Golf, aggravated in no small measure by what are considered to be much too severe penalties for trivial offences. The golfer is an honest man, but the imposition of such penalties as "Loss of Hole" by the opponent if he is hit by the player's ball would infer that if the Rules were made for honest men the penalties were most decidedly imposed to guard against dishonesty.

Several of the rules have been written in simpler form as experience on the Sub-Committee appointed to answer questions showed me that a large majority of questions came from [club] Committees who could not understand the meaning behind the rule. The Rules of Golf are not meant to create quibbles as to the shade of meaning of certain phrases.

Anyone who studies the Decisions of the R. & A. over the past few years since the introduction of the present code will be inclined to the view that the situation is much the same as that suggested in the second paragraph of the above quotation.

The Lindsay-Buchanan code was not that finally evolved, because while the 1950-1 rules incorporated the idea of less severe penalties, they also followed the American pattern of combined rules for match- and medal-play, which Colonel Lindsay and Mr. Buchanan considered unsuitable.

Mr. Bernard Darwin was chairman of the Rules of Golf Committee responsible for the new code, and here are some of his observations in the Preface published on January 1, 1950:

The Rules of Golf have been revised by the Royal and Ancient Golf Club of St. Andrews with the object of simplifying their interpretation. The revision is based largely on experience gained from questions asked and decisions given during the past fifteen years.

The most important individual change made is in regard to the reduction in penalty for the ball lost, out of bounds or unplayable, and the consequent general reduction in penalties which this change has entailed. A referendum was held among members of the Royal and Ancient Golf Club as to whether the penalty in each case should be as before, loss of stroke and distance, or loss of distance only. The opinion of the governing bodies at home and overseas was also requested on this point. In each case there was a majority in favour of distance only.

It was therefore decided to give effect to the majority's view and, at the same time, for the sake of consistency, to reduce the penalties in the other rules proportionately. The penalty for all breaches of rule, except those which must be regarded as deliberate and therefore inexcusable, is now one stroke in both match- and medal-play. . . .

It has been decided not to alter the rule as to what is commonly known as the Stymie since the majority of the Governing Bodies consulted were in favour of retaining the existing rule.

These rules will remain unaltered for two years. At the end of that period they will be reconsidered and amended if necessary. It is hoped that this will result in a code which will require no further alteration for many years.

But the months immediately preceding the ratification of the 1950 code by St. Andrews had seen a great deal of argument, and opposition from some of Mr. Darwin's contemporaries was very strong. To a traditionalist of his character it must have been a sore tussle between his loyalty to the Committee of which he was chairman and his own deep-rooted feelings about how the game should be played.

The views of Mr. Robert Harris, the 1923 Amateur Champion, could be expressed without equivocation because his membership of the Rules of Golf Committee had ended in 1946 after nearly twenty years' service, and he was free to go into the battle wholeheartedly on the side of tradition.

Soon after the circulation of the proposed code to members of the R. & A., early in 1949, he published a treatise describing the new rules as "a threat to the game."

Here are some of his comments:

Many will wonder why such vital changes are considered necessary since the present rules have operated so smoothly for the game, and so efficiently in championships and other important competitions. The small number of pertinent queries submitted to the Rules of Golf Committee during the past fifteen years showed that the present code was understood by, and agreeable to all, and was universally accepted in the right spirit.

This proposed new code should be carefully studied by all true golfers since its main purport is to reduce the game to a level of easy going in the softening of its difficulties by the wholesale reduction of penalties for inefficient play.

In fact, it creates a new and different game. In sequence, form and wording it is complicated and confusing, and golfers accustomed to the old familiar terms would have difficulty in understanding it without a course of special study.

It sets out to mollify the sporting aspect in golf by a wholesale reduction of penalties for inefficient play, for carelessness and bad manners, and if passed will effectively undermine the very fundamentals of the game besides entirely destroying that feeling which inspires all real golfers to exert their best efforts in the face of difficulties.

This proposed remission and assimilation of penalties is being put forward as the result of a plebiscite by postal vote taken from the members of the R. & A. and outside Societies or Unions, an entirely unconstitutional method of deciding a change in the Rules of Golf.

The result of the referendum showed a vote which

would be inadequate to carry a straight motion properly put to the Royal and Ancient Club at a general meeting and voted on in accordance with the Rules of the club. On this spurious plebiscite vote the Rules of Golf Committee have assumed a mandate to propose a general reduction of penalties throughout the game on the slender plea of attaining consistency. Apparently there is a lack of confidence in the Committee about these softening changes. The code is to be regarded as merely temporary with the promise of a revision in two years' time.

It will indeed be a herculean task then to unscramble the omelette with so many different codes coming into operation throughout this country and the world.

Mr. Harris was no doubt right about the Committee lacking confidence in its own production, but he was pessimistic about the job of "unscrambling the omelette." It was unscrambled by the process of adding it to the American omelette and getting all the best cooks around the kitchen table to evolve a new dish.

This plan took shape during the first year of the British 1950 code, for not many months passed before the experiences of golfers everywhere proved Mr. Harris's contention that the experimental rules undermined the fundamentals of the game. As already related, the R. & A. and the U.S.G.A. got together in the spring of 1951 and the present code was born.

Unfortunately, in the rebound from the extreme lenience of the experimental code the golf world gained international agreement but lost a great opportunity of producing a common code for the common golfer.

Whether that opportunity will ever recur is a matter for conjecture, but if and when it does, no pains should be spared to grab the chance.

CHAPTER III

It All Began with Feathers

BEING the most important item in the game, the ball is naturally mentioned more often in the rules than any other item. Indeed, of more than 600 references in the index nearly half refer to the small white object which all golfers would like to propel 250 yards in a straight line, but which defies the efforts of the great majority to do so.

There have been many varieties of golf ball—the featherie, the guttie, the rubber-core, the floater, the bramble, the recess, the mesh, and the dimple—to say nothing of Cunobelin's pebble.

In its abstract form—abstract with human connections—the ball can also be known as lost, unplayable, out of bounds, and provisional, but in this chapter we are concerned with the ball as a hard fact.

For all its apparent solidity, however, the golf

ball is endowed with life and sensitivity. Around the core, usually a rubber pad containing paste or liquid, are wound lengths of rubber tape and thread. When the appropriate size has been reached and the ball is looking rather like a ball of Mother's knitting-wool wound too tightly by Father, it is encased in a cover stamped with the requisite patterns, painted in glossy white, and given numbers, coloured dots, playing-card symbols according to the makers' fancy.

And all of it—core, windings, cover, paint, spots, and numbers—must weigh not more than 1.62 ounces or have a diameter of less than 1.62 inches (1.68 inches in the United States and Canada).

The golfer should be aware of these vital statistics so that the next time he takes a ball out of the bag and tosses the wrapping-paper into the tee-box (we hope) with the air of a millionaire throwing away a fiver, he will have a proper respect for the lively, eager piece of mechanism which some heavy-handed lout is about to slice into the pond.

Little wonder that the proud, glistening object, stripped naked and placed shivering on a tee-peg, will deliberately steer itself into the pond, preferring a watery grave to the disgrace and indignity of being topped, hacked, whacked, sliced, and pulled through gorse, rough, and bunkers for eighteen agonizing holes.

It may be asked why a missile made with such precision and having so constant a centre of gravity should play such tricks. The reason is—spin, which makes a golf ball react, sometimes violently, to the misapplication of external force.

There are three main types of spin—top-spin, under-spin, and lateral-spin. Lateral-spin can operate either clockwise or anti-clockwise but seldom in both wises at once, although Colonel Foozlequik might be suspected of achieving this when he hits a low shot over the left-hand rough which finishes in a bunker on the right of the fairway.

The experts agree that under-spin is the most common, but handicap golfers know this to be the opposite of the truth. The average golf ball is propelled with top-spin and, although the experts maintain it is most difficult to hit a ball that way, thousands of amateurs up and down the country know it is the easiest thing in the world.

The aforementioned Colonel, for example, specializes in various elegant types of top-spin, beginning with a complete air shot with the driver, continuing with a slashing brassie shot which nicks a little paint off the ball, and ending with a nice low mashie-niblick stroke which sends the ball trickling up to the pin, where it rolls over gently and smiles maliciously through a gashed cover at the Colonel's astounded and discomfited opponent.

Indeed, when you consider the golfers in the field, and how they spin, it becomes obvious that Ryder Cup players, in all their glory, play some entirely different game.

But the golf ball, whether it spins right, left,

under, or over, is the same for everyone. It leaves its cover hoping for the best, expecting the worst—and usually getting it—and must sometimes envy its humble predecessors, the featherie and the guttie, which had quick ways out of the ordeal.

The stitched leather casing stuffed with soft feathers which served the lairds of Fife more than a century ago was wont to take advantage of a rainstorm to become sodden and virtually immovable, or would burst from an ill-timed blow with a cleek and ooze feathers through the gash.

The guttie had a habit of breaking into halves or even smaller pieces when it had had enough of being belaboured all over the course, but the pieces could be melted down again and reincarnation achieved.

It is to the guttie, by the way, that we owe the patterns on the modern golf ball. The first gutties were made smooth like billiard balls, and aroused much scorn and ridicule among the feather-ball makers because they were inferior in behaviour and ducked to earth like shot partridges after travelling about fifty yards.

It was then discovered that much-used balls, bearing the marks of damage from club-heads and other causes, flew better than new ones, and the great truth dawned. The more dents and cuts a ball had, the better it behaved (thus proving the widely held theory of the time, since abandoned, that corporal punishment made good citizens).

So the new balls from the mould were laboriously nicked by hammers, until the patterned mould was evolved.

If we are to believe Greek mythology, the idea of a spherical object in use for recreation must have been very ancient, and we can take Homer's word for it with all the more confidence since we know from boyhood experiences that the instinct to throw a ball is fundamental.

In more recent times the organization of games has become more complex, and each game has developed its own equiment. With golfers, as with the players of other contemporary games, it was merely a question of getting the right ball for the job, and in the production of such balls in the early days no one worried about standards of size or performance.

The early feather-stuffed balls in use at the time the modern history of golf began were made from segments of leather stitched together except for one opening, into which were shovelled and shoved as many boiled feathers as could be crammed by manual strength and skill. I always think no description of the making of a "featherie" could be better than that of the oft-quoted Thomas Mathieson, the Edinburgh lawyer-turned-clergyman, in his poem "The Goff." Of the famous ball-maker of the time, Bobson, he writes:

> Who, with matchless art,
> Shapes the firm hide, connecting every part,

Then in a socket sets the well-stitched void
And through the eyelet drives the downy tide;
Crowds urging crowds the forceful brogue impels.
The feathers harden and the leather swells;
He crams and sweats, yet crams and urges more
Till scarce the turgid globe contains its store.

Now Bobson, or any other ball-maker of his time, might make a dozen balls which, if put through calipers and weighed, would be found different from each other in both factors.

But there would have been a rough-and-ready approximation in the size of the leather segments, and when the gutta-percha ball was introduced, it was natural that the new balls, made much more easily and cheaper than the featheries, should be moulded in the size which golfers had found most suitable. The weight, of course, was governed by the size, since the material was solid gutta-percha.

At the time of the introduction of the guttie, in 1848, the golf-ball trade had its headquarters at St. Andrews, where the chief maker was Allan Robertson, the champion golfer of the day, who employed Tom Morris and was afterwards in partnership with him.

Some idea of the labour involved in making featheries, and some explanation of the high cost, may be gained from the fact that, according to a contemporary account, it was considered remarkable evidence of the development of golf that in Allan's shop alone 2,456 feather balls were made in 1844, an advance of fifty per cent over the total of three years earlier. Golf in those days, at any rate if played with what passed for the proper equipment, was a game only for the well-to-do classes.

The coming of the guttie changed all that. Allan Robertson might look glum and defend his trade in featheries to the last pinion, but there was no answer to the solid spheres of gutta-percha which came tumbling from the moulds and, when damaged or misshapen, could be restored to mint condition by warming, remoulding, and repainting.

Apart from giving a tremendous impulse to golf by ensuring a vast reduction in costs and a corresponding increase in the number of balls produced, the use of gutta-percha had a distinct influence on the progress towards standardization, although official control was still many years away. The feather-ball-maker, sweating and gasping away with socket, rammer, and awl, was content merely to fill the cavity to bursting-point. But the maker of the guttie had a mould which turned out ball after ball of identical size and weight. To be sure, there were moulds of slightly different sizes and in time there were several different makes of ball on the market. But a golfer using a ball of 29 dwt. was not disturbed if his opponent used one of 26 dwt. or any of the half-sizes in between. It was an age when golfers pleased themselves and authority had not yet thought of limits.

Then, in 1902, the Haskell rubber-cored ball

appeared. It was invented in the United States and
introduced in Britain just prior to the Open Championship of that year at Hoylake. None of the professionals competing had tried the new ball, but one
of them, the late Alexander Herd, was playing with
the great Hoylake amateur John Ball in a practice
round. Herd was being consistently outdriven by
Ball, using a Haskell. The professional was suitably
impressed, was invited to try the ball, and lost no
time in buying some. He won the championship, and
that was good enough to end half a century of guttie-
dom.

As with the change from featherie to guttie, the
transition from guttie to rubber-core meant a big
advance in performance and consequently a greater
need for some form of standardization.

For some time there was no official action, but
the situation soon developed to a point where some
form of control became essential. The main reason
was that the rubber-core, consisting of windings of
rubber thread over a volatile centre, was much more
susceptible than the guttie had been to manufactur-
ing improvements.

One and a half ounces of gutta-percha ejected
from a mould was just a lump of gutta-percha, but
the rubber-core was different, and the Edwardian
era was notable for an intensive war among manufacturers, all claiming great performances and long distances for their various products.

Commercial rivalry in itself was not bad because

it tended to improve the quality of the products, but the campaign for distance was creating a situation in which courses were in danger of becoming out of date and the game in danger of being ruined.

In 1912 the Royal and Ancient Golf Club acted, not without murmurs from the United States but with the full support of the trade in Great Britain, who agreed to certain means of limiting the performance of the ball. There still remained in production, however, a variety of different weights, and even up to the end of the 1914-18 war there were at least four recognized weights—the floater (27 dwt.) and non-floaters at 29, 30, and 31 dwt.

With the end of the war came the need to get some form of standardization. In 1919 the Rules of Golf Committee stated they were of the opinion that, to preserve the balance between the power of the ball and length of the holes, and to "retain the special features of the game," the power of the ball should be limited; and therefore they intended to consult the U.S.G.A. and other interested bodies before making any concrete proposal.

Early in 1920 it was reported that the U.S.G.A. were in full agreement with the Committee that the player and not the inventor should guide the development of the game.

Discussions between U.S.G.A. and R. & A. representatives, in which delegates from Canada and South Africa took part, were held in 1920 at Muirfield and in London. It was agreed (and subsequently ratified by the two governing bodies): "That on and after May 1st, 1921, the weight of the ball shall not be greater than 1.62 ounces and the size not less than 1.62 inches in diameter."

It was added that the authorities of both Great Britain and the United States would take whatever steps thought necessary to limit the power of the ball, should any ball of greater power be introduced.

From that time onwards there was clear evidence that there could never be complete and lasting agreement between America and Britain over the dimensions of the ball. Within two or three years of the 1920 discussions it was apparent that the Americans wanted a larger and lighter ball, and there were indeed American experiments with a ball not less than 1.68 inches and not more than 1.55 ounces. There was some idea of testing such a ball in the Amateur and Open Championships of 1926 in Britain, but it was turned down for a very good reason, that such important events ought not to be the subject of experiment.

That was the year that Bobby Jones had the historic 36-holes total of 134 in the Southern qualifying rounds of the Open Championship at Sunningdale, including a second round of 66 often described as one of the most perfect rounds of golf ever played. It is a matter for conjecture what score he would have made with a ball six hundredths of an inch wider and seven hundredths of an ounce lighter.

In 1928 the Rules of Golf Committee suggested adopting a ball of the experimental American dimensions, but this time the U.S.G.A. asked for a postponement pending further experiments. One year later the U.S.G.A. took unilateral action by announcing their intention to introduce on January 1, 1931, a ball not less than 1.68 inches in diameter and not heavier than 1.55 ounces. This was described as "an easier and pleasanter ball for the average golfer," but it lasted only one year. On January 1, 1932, the U.S. specification became 1.68 inches and 1.62 ounces, and so it has remained.

The general rules revision of 1934 included no change in the British dimensions, but subsequent events indicated that but for the outbreak of the 1939 war there might have been an alteration. In 1938 the British Golf Unions and Empire governing bodies had been asked by St. Andrews for their views "concerning the introduction of a golf ball which would have the effect of reducing the distances obtained." Whatever evidence was collected on that point was pigeon-holed and never revealed by the R. & A. until, in 1945, following much press comment on the possibility of a change, St. Andrews issued a statement including this paragraph:

The question of a standard ball has been under careful consideration for twenty years and all the tests which have been carried out by scientists, by the use of special instruments, by golf-ball manufacturers, and by golfers have been analysed by a Sub-Committee of the Rules of Golf Committee. As a result the specification for a standard golf ball is now being examined. A decision has not been made, nor can one be made until the Sub-Committee completes its report and until all the details and views of the representative authorities are laid before and studied by a full meeting of the Rules of Golf Committee.

In the letter of 1938 to the golf unions at home and overseas the Rules of Golf Committee expressed the opinion that the adoption of a less powerful golf ball would be to the advantage of all grades of golfers, and there is no doubt that the golf-ball sub-committee had this in mind when proposing, at the May 1946 Business Meeting of the R. & A., that "the weight of the ball shall not be greater than 1.62 ounces and the size of the ball not be less than 1.62 inches in diameter."

But at that meeting there were many members ready to point out that much water had flowed under the Swilcan Bridge since 1939, that the opinions of the various unions might have changed in the meantime, and that in any case it was perhaps not in the best interest of the golfing industry, getting back into production after the war, to ask manufacturers to undertake the mechanical changes which an altered specification would make necessary.

So it was agreed to postpone any consideration

of a new ball for three years, and by tacit agreement the matter has been left there.

It seems that by this time St. Andrews had become convinced that, so far as the ball was concerned, the paths of the United States and Great Britain would always diverge. In 1951, during the discussions which led to the re-unification of the American and British rules, it was suggested as a way out of the ball impasse that both sizes of ball be made legal in all countries. This proposal was agreed to by the joint Anglo-American committee but not ratified by the U.S.G.A., presumably because there was no disposition to give American golfers the option and so create a situation which might affect the American golf-ball industry.

Whatever the reason, the U.S.G.A. sugared the pill of rejection by conceding that international teams playing in the United States would be allowed to use the small British ball if they so desired.

Thus was removed the only serious disadvantage of the discrepancy in sizes, and no doubt the concession postponed still further any definite move towards changing the British specification. The Golf Ball Sub-Committee of the Rules of Golf Committee still exists under the name of Ball and Implements Sub-Committee, and the question of golf-ball development is kept under constant review by the Rules of Golf Committee and the U.S.G.A. But the ordinary golfer is neither aware of these activities nor interested in them.

He now uses a ball which will travel 250 yards if well struck and 150 yards or more even when half-topped. So far as he is concerned, it is "an easy and pleasant ball," and the only change in which he is likely to be the least bit interested is a change in price.

CHAPTER IV

From Blackthorn to Steel Shaft

IT HAS already been shown how the spread in popularity of golf made necessary a corresponding increase in the number and verbiosity of the rules; and how for this reason, as well as because of advances in science and technology, the authorities were obliged to control the power of the golf ball.

During the same period there were parallel developments in the design and quality of golf clubs, and therefore parallel moves to keep these, too, under official control.

Prior to the introduction of the R. & A. code of 1902 there had been no obvious tendency among golfers to depart from "traditional form and make" so far as clubs were concerned.

For at least two centuries there had been a generally accepted specification, vague at first and later more detailed, as essentially a stick bent or

Old golf balls in the museum of the Royal Wimbledon Golf
Club. Typical feather-stuffed balls made more than a century ago. The cases were formed by segments of leather
stitched together except for one opening, through which
feathers—traditionally as many as would fill a top hat—
were stuffed. Before the case was stuffed, the feathers were
boiled to break up the pinions and facilitate stuffing. The
picture shows clearly how feather balls varied in size.

Left to right: a hand-made gutta-percha ball dating from
the latter half of the nineteenth century; one of the early
Haskells (*circa* 1903); and a comparatively modern rubber-
core ball used by the Captain of the Royal Wimbledon
Club when opening the new course in 1924.

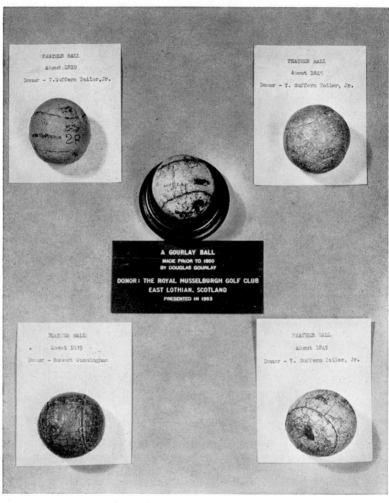

Here is an exhibit from the U.S.G.A Golf Museum and Library at Golf House, New York, which takes us back to the days of the "featheries." Douglas Gourlay was one of the leading makers of the early golf ball, constructed from a stitched hide cover stuffed to bursting-point with boiled feathers.

curved at the striking end, with that end constructed in such a way that it presented a flat surface to the ball.

In the very early days—and I am now thinking not so much of Ancient Britain as of fifteenth-century Scotland—such implements must have ranged from the primitive cudgel cut from the hedgerow to the better-finished article made by local craftsmen from local material, but still rude in appearance and clumsy in performance when compared with present-day clubs.

The age of primitive clubs, however, did not depart with the rise of the great club-makers of the seventeenth and eighteenth centuries, for we have evidence that more than one giant of the game known to golfers of the past two generations was accustomed in his youth to play golf by improvisation.

Sandy Herd, the 1902 Open Champion, used to cut jointed stumps from the woods around St. Andrews to make rough clubheads, so that he and his boyhood friends could strike "balls" made from champagne corks weighted with nails.

And Harry Vardon, six times Open Champion, started playing golf in his native Jersey with clubs made from oak and blackthorn. Heads were made from short lengths of oak branches and shafts from the blackthorn, a circumstance which, as Harry's brother Tom has pointed out, was responsible for a peculiarity of the famous "Vardon grip."

When the Vardon brothers were becoming prominent they were criticized because, instead of wrapping the thumbs round the shaft, they held the thumbs down the shaft. This method soon came to be recognized as effective, but it was adopted by the Vardons not from a conscious sense of its value but from sheer necessity.

For the blackthorn in its natural state was plentifully carbuncled with knots and lumps, and the lads of Grouville placed both thumbs down the shaft to avoid the soreness and blistering which would have resulted from adopting what was then the orthodox grip.

From such small things great truths emerge.

But there are no longer piles of champagne corks outside the Royal and Ancient clubhouse, small boys no longer cut clubs from the virgin wood, and the age of improvisation has departed to leave the game, as well as the modern father, all the poorer. Nevertheless, these pieces of history remain to remind us of the free-and-easy days when golfers could please themselves to almost any extent about the missiles they used and the means they employed for propelling them.

The primitive age of golf can be said to extend from our mythical Cunobelin to the early part of the second millennium. We can imagine that Cunobelin and Caractacus, after their little argument had been settled, were not long content with the equipment with which they had started, and must soon have realized that a cudgel thin at one end and bulbous at the other, studded with flints, was not the ideal implement.

Centuries afterwards someone, not a golfer, was to describe the game as "hitting a small ball into a small hole with implements singularly ill-adapted to the purpose." That is no doubt what Cunobelin and Caractacus thought about their clubs. They were admirable for coshing a bear on the head or cracking the skull of an enemy, but singularly ill-adapted to hitting a pebble, apart from the fact that the pebble itself was singularly ill-adapted to accurate flight.

A smaller head flattened on the striking side and without flints would be admirable, and our pioneers would search the forest for handy sticks of the right proportions and shape. The blackthorn and the oak and the ash would provide them with raw materials, and we can imagine them getting to work with fire and leather thongs and knives to fashion the first golf clubs, with no trouble about purchase tax or the regulations on "form and make."

No doubt Cunobelin and Sandy Herd had a lot in (as well as off the) common.

Although the use of a naturally curved or angular stick cut from growing wood must have been the origin of the golf club, some disadvantages would become apparent with the growth of the game into a regular pastime. It would, for instance, be difficult to cut a stick precisely suited to the purpose, the bend being too slight or too pronounced or the angle of branch with stem being too acute or too obtuse.

In any case, without some strengthening at the bend, the stick would not stand many vigorous contacts with ground or ball.

Sticks of this kind were cut from hedges by the club-makers of two centuries ago—not for use as complete clubs, but only for the heads of clubs. The trunk of the hedge-shoot protruded horizontally and then shot upwards, and the thick horizontal part was used for the heads. They were shaped and joined to a straight stick, and so it was possible for the early club-makers not only to produce by splicing and binding a strong club, but also to control the angle between shaft and head. That was the birth of golf-club-making as an art, and the real foundation of the industry of today.

How early this fundamental departure was made we do not know, but, as Sir Guy Campbell has pointed out, there is evidence from documents and paintings of clubs existing in the fifteenth century that they were basically similar to those of the nineteenth century now to be seen in golf-club museums.

There was a club-maker (unnamed) at Perth who supplied clubs to James IV of Scotland (1473–1513), and in 1603, on the accession of James VI of Scotland to the throne of England, we have the first reference by name of a club-maker. He was William Mayne, "bower burges of Edinburgh," who was appointed by Royal Warrant "bower, clubmaker and speirmaker to his Heines."

It was from William Mayne and the unknown club-maker of Perth that the ancient art of club-making descended to those craftsmen of whose work samples still exist—Simon Cossar, Hugh Philp, Douglas McEwen, and the rest.

By the time these artists were established at their various centres, club-making had been following certain well-defined lines for many years. And since golfing communities were few and compact and club-makers worked in the centre of those communities and were in constant association with the ideas and wishes of players, the "form and make" became standardized without need of official action, even if any one authority in those days could have had the power to act.

In fact the design and manufacture of golf clubs developed untrammelled by official interference until the beginning of the present century, and from the terms of the restriction incorporated in the new code of rules introduced in 1907 we are led to form a very poor opinion of the morals of golfers who had come into the game.

The Rules of Golf Committee [ran the stricture] intimates that it will not sanction any substantial departure from the traditional and accepted form and make of golf clubs which, in its opinion, consist of a plain shaft and a head which does not contain any mechanical contrivance, such as springs.

Three years later, having received several queries, the Committee added these words:

The Committee also regards as illegal the use of such clubs as those of the mallet-headed type or such clubs as have the neck so bent as to produce a similar effect.

Although the 1907 rules were made in consultation with America and were intended to apply to both countries and indeed to the whole world of golf, this ban on the "mallet-headed" putter nearly brought about a schism between the Royal and Ancient Golf Club and the United States Golf Association. In fact, the opposition of the R. & A. to "mallet-headed" clubs had sprung from the use by an American of a club of that type.

Walter J. Travis, Australian-born but resident in the United States for many years, had won the U. S. Amateur Championship three times and was the current holder when, in 1904, he paid his first visit to Britain.

The Amateur Championship of that year was played at Sandwich, and Travis, who had previously visited St. Andrews and North Berwick to get experience of seaside links, showed very poor form at those places, being particularly disappointed with his putting, usually the strong part of his game.

On arriving at Sandwich he was offered the loan of a putter of curious design, at any rate to British eyes. It was the property of another American entrant, and Travis did so well with it that it is not too much to say he won the championship by his putting.

But the fact that he had won with a club of unusual and indeed revolutionary design was enough to set the heads wagging. The putter was a rectangular piece of wood with straight sides, and the shaft set vertically in the centre. From the place of its origin it was called the Schenectady Putter, and it was a type of centre-shafted putter.

We all know the centre-shafted putter is now legal, but at that time there was a very strong prejudice against departures from "traditional form and make," and there is no doubt that much of that feeling sprang from the visit of Travis and his friend's Schenectady in 1904. Not because he won, but because he used a club which offended the natural conservatism of British golfers.

Whatever the reasons behind the ban, it is certain that when the Rules of Golf Committee set their faces so resolutely against "mallet-headed" clubs the golfers of Great Britain and the United States came nearer than before or since to breaking apart.

For some time there had been signs of differing views springing not only from the different conditions under which golf was played in the United States, but also from a natural tendency on the part of the Americans towards the idea that they should have matters their own way in their own country.

The seeds of golf in America were sown by immigrants from Scotland, but the plant grew strongly in American soil and was nourished by the quick-action fertilizers of a new, vigorous, and enterprising community.

On the other hand, the American golf pioneers were obliged at first to play under the rules as laid down by St. Andrews, and, however much the progressive spirits of the United States Golf Association (formed in 1894) might rankle under this necessity, there was no alternative except to break away from St. Andrews and lead an independent existence.

This desire for independence was shown clearly in the early years of the U.S.G.A., for although Charles B. Macdonald and Lawrence Curtis, appointed in 1897 to interpret the rules of golf, recommended no change in the Royal and Ancient code, they did add what were termed "rulings of the U.S.G.A."

Four years later the President of the U.S.G.A., Mr. R. H. Robertson, made virtually a Declaration of Independence when he said:

I think we should guard against being too much restricted and held down by precedent and tradition. I fear that is the fault of the game on the other side. Do not let us be afraid of innovations simply because they are innovations. Nothing can come to America and stay very long without being Americanized in character; and I hope the game will be no exception to this rule. I should like to see American golf.

56

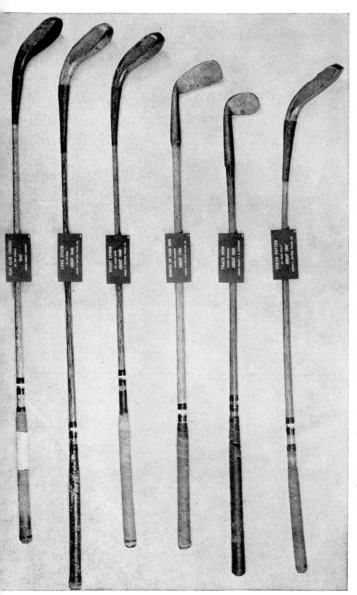

Mis-hitting a feather-stuffed ball with an iron club was likely to cause a split in the leather cover. Therefore most clubs of the feather-ball period, as this exhibit in the U.S.G.A Golf Museum shows, had wooden heads. Iron-headed clubs were used for such special purposes as getting the ball out of ruts (second from bottom) and from bunkers (third from bottom).

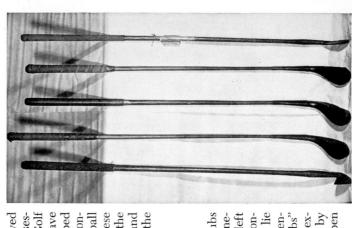

LEFT: Some ancient clubs, believed to be of Dutch origin, in the possession of the Royal Wimbledon Golf Club. The two on the right have concave faces; the curiously shaped one on the extreme left, also concave, was used for getting the ball out of serious trouble. Most of these clubs, and particularly that in the centre, are extremely heavy, and impossible to swing as fully as the modern club is swung.

RIGHT: Essentially British clubs made in the style of the early nineteenth century. On the extreme left is a short-bladed rut-iron with a concave face, used whenever the lie precluded the use of the wooden-headed flat-soled "play clubs" (shown in the centre). On the extreme right is a driving-iron used by Tom Kidd, who won the Open Championship in 1873.

It was obvious that American golfers would shortly be prepared to formulate their own rules if necessary, but they took what might be called a constitutional step in 1907 by demanding a revision of the St. Andrews rules.

In this the U.S.G.A. had support from other parts of the golfing world, and since the wisest counsels prevailed at St. Andrews, the necessary steps were soon in motion.

The Rules of Golf Committee not only agreed to set about a revision, but also invited Mr. Macdonald to fill the first vacancy on the Committee.

The U.S.G.A. sent to St. Andrews a draft code embodying their views. Some of the new suggestions were adopted by St. Andrews and some rejected, but Captain W. H. Burn, then Chairman of the Rules of Golf Committee, expressed the hope that the U.S.G.A. would be satisfied with the new code and with the consideration given to the American views.

It can be assumed that the U.S.G.A. were satisfied with the new clause concerning form and make of golf clubs; indeed, it was most probably one of the suggestions included in the U.S.G.A. draft. But they were clearly appalled by the implications of the addition in 1910 about "mallet-headed" putters, and there was open revolt when Captain Burn, being asked for clarification, indicated that the Royal and Ancient considered the Schenectady putter to be of the mallet-headed type.

57

But in this crisis St. Andrews, and indeed the whole world of golf, had a friend at court, and to his attitude and actions must be credited the preservation of unity. The peacemaker was Mr. Macdonald, whose inclusion on the Rules of Golf Committee was due not only to his undoubted interest in Anglo-American relations, but also to the fact that he had more than a tenuous acquaintance with St. Andrews and its traditions.

At the age of sixteen Mr. Macdonald, who was born on the Canadian side of Niagara Falls, had the good fortune to be sent to Scotland to continue his studies at St. Andrews University, and it was during his sojourn in the "auld grey toon" that he became interested in the art.

On his return to America he was apparently too busy to have much time for developing his game, and in fact did not take up golf seriously until the age of thirty-eight, when he helped to found the Chicago Golf Club. Two years later, in 1895, Mr Macdonald won the first American Amateur Championship to be held under the auspices of the U.S.G.A., and thereafter he was a regular golfer and, what was more important, an enthusiastic administrator.

And it was against this background that Mr. Macdonald, now an elder statesman of fifty-five, entered the role of peacemaker between the R. & A. and the U.S.G.A.

First he sent a remonstrating letter to St. Andrews pointing out that the Schenectady and the wry-necked putter, also under ban, had been accepted by Americans for ten years and were used by fifty per cent of American golfers.

He added that he had suggested to the U.S.G.A. Rules Committee that under Section 10 of the U.S.G.A. bylaws they were permitted to interpret the St. Andrews rules to suit American conditions. There was nothing, in his view, to prevent the U.S.G.A. from adopting the St. Andrews clause but interpreting it so as not to bar the Schenectady.

This will, I think, obviate a distinct breach [continued Mr. Macdonald]. For my part I do not think the Schenectady is a mallet. Neither is a wry-necked putter. Neither of these clubs really makes the slightest difference to a man's play. It is only his character of mind. Travis is now putting with a Braid aluminium and if anything putting better than ever.

After alluding to the "unique position" of the Royal and Ancient Golf Club in commanding an allegiance throughout the world of golf, Mr. Macdonald concluded:

A regime so honourably and effectively administered in a game that encircles the world, appealing to all classes, should to my mind be conserved with the utmost care and delicacy, and it would be a source of the deepest regret should that allegiance be jeopardized by so small and unnecessary a matter as the interpretation of the word "mallet," which means nothing to the game itself.

59

The addition in 1910 of the ban on "mallet-headed" clubs had been inspired by a question from the Nga Motu club of New Zealand and another from Pickeridge Golf Club. The New Zealand query was: "With regard to Form and Make of Golf Clubs is it permissible to use a small croquet mallet to putt with?"

Answer: "A croquet mallet is not a golf club and is inadmissible."

When the Pickeridge club cited the case of a competitor who had used a putter "made in the form of a croquet mallet" the Rules of Golf Committee not only confirmed that he should be disqualified but roused themselves to the following extent:

The Rules of Golf Committee is of opinion that the time has come for the Royal and Ancient Golf Club to decide at a General Meeting whether the various mallet-headed implements at present in use are to be permitted or not. The Rules of Golf Committee is also of the opinion that it is not allowable to employ the vertical croquet stroke as a method of putting. The Committee considers that it is much to be deplored that players, instead of trying to master the use of golf clubs, should endeavour to overcome the difficulties of the game by using implements which were never associated with it.

This ascetic attitude has not been maintained, of course, and nowadays the centre-shafted putter is in universal use and several celebrated golfers, including champions of both sexes, a former Walker

Cup captain, and a captain of the Royal and Ancient Golf Club, have straddled over the ball and putted croquet-fashion.

But in 1909 St. Andrews was high-minded on this subject, which will explain why, despite the Macdonald letter, they emphasized disagreement with American opinion by incorporating the ban on mallet-headed putters in the "form and make" clause.

Once more there was danger of schism, and once more Macdonald the Peacemaker poured the oil. At the General Meeting of the U.S.G.A. in January 1911 he pleaded for "unification," asked the U.S.G.A. to go on co-operating with St. Andrews, and reiterated his opinion that Section 10 of the U.S.G.A. constitution "covers it all."

The U.S.G.A. voted to accept the St. Andrews revision, but also to invoke Bylaw 10 and continue to allow the use of the Schenectady Putter under their jurisdiction.

So the danger point was passed with the U.S.G.A. and St. Andrews agreeing to differ, but from that time forth the Americans did not scruple to go their own way whenever they deemed it necessary—as, for example, in the cases of the stymie and steel shafts. Indeed, at one time their rules were completely different from those of St. Andrews. But that was merely a passing phase, and now amity, fostered by a more liberal outlook and a more democratic composition of the Rules of Golf Committee, reigns among golfers everywhere.

Fifteen years after this amicable settlement of
the "mallet-headed" dispute the progressive spirit of
the U.S.G.A. was seen again over the question of
steel shafts. For some time manufacturers in the
United States had been experimenting with tubular
steel shafts, and in keeping with tradition St. Andrews looked askance at this tendency to drift away
from hickory.

And when the U.S.G.A. decided in 1926 to
legalize steel shafts they acted alone, St. Andrews
holding out for three years despite efforts by the
trade to persuade them otherwise.

So early as 1923 one firm had devised a club
shaft made from sections of split bamboo and, on the
grounds that hickory was getting scarce, asked St.
Andrews to legalize it, without success.

After the unilateral action of the U.S.G.A. a renewed attempt was made to win over St. Andrews,
but the Rules of Golf Committee did not agree there
was a shortage of hickory and were supported by the
Professional Golfers' Association of Great Britain,
who stated that the introduction of steel shafts would
be "detrimental to the professional trade in the country."

There was the crux of the matter. It was the old
story of progressive versus conservative thought as
we had seen in the transition from feather-ball to
guttie and from guttie to rubber-core. At the time of
the disagreement over steel shafts there were many
factory-made clubs on the market, but most of the

golf-club trade in Britain was still in the hands of professionals making and copying clubs at their own benches. The majority of them could not visualize how much advantage they would gain from the sale of factory-made clubs with steel shafts. They could see only the possibility of their busy workshops being silent and a big change in the conditions they had known all their lives.

Now, more than twenty years afterwards, we know that the steel shaft was a necessity. Apart from making up for the growing world shortage of hickory, it helped to speed up production and, above all, made possible the manufacture of clubs in matched sets. In no other way, certainly not by the maintenance of individual craftsmen's shops scattered over the country, could the great public demand for golf equipment have been met.

For some time after St. Andrews fell into line and legalized steel shafts there were moves on both sides of the Atlantic aimed at constraining the ingenuity and inventiveness of individual makers and the big firms, but, however much the U.S.G.A. and the R. & A. co-operated to preserve the traditional form and make of wood and iron clubs, there was still the gulf between them on the subject of putters. Indeed, when the R. & A. issued their experimental code in 1949 it included in the very first rule a statement that "the mallet-headed type of club, or club with neck so bent as to produce a similar effect, is illegal."

Golfers at Law

Two years later this long-standing ban was removed in a curiously oblique manner. After detailing that the shaft of a club shall be fixed to the clubhead at the heel, Rule 2 adds this qualification: "However, the shaft of a putter may be fixed at any point in the head."

In the present code this addition becomes an "Exception to Rule," and, furthermore, a putter is defined as a club "designed primarily for use on a putting-green."

There is a certain concession to progressive thought about all this which seems somehow typical of a state of mind which has converted the rules from what, half a century ago, were rules for honest men into a code for criminals.

It reveals an underlying suspicion that if the modern golfer is given more than an inch in the matter of the centre-shafted putter he will take a yard and equip all his clubs with centre shafts and call them all putters, at whatever cost to his game.

Of course a putter is a club designed for use on a putting-green. Could one drive with a centre-shafted putter? And if one could, would one?

However much the Royal and Ancient lagged behind the U.S.G.A. on steel shafts, however divergent the two views were about putters, there was unquestioned unanimity about the basic principles of form and make—"a plain shaft and a head which does not contain any mechanical contrivances such as springs."

64

In its early form the clause did not go beyond that injunction, but more legislation became necessary because of a tendency, most marked among American golfers, to use iron clubs having faces designed or converted to increase the amount of spin imparted to the ball.

There was considerable comment during the Open Championship of 1921 at St. Andrews about the lofted clubs used by the winner, Jock Hutchison. In particular he used a mashie which not only had deep lines in the face but was capable of being intensified in its effect by the use of a file. I was not at this championship, but a colleague who was told me that during the replay, in which Hutchison beat Roger Wethered, the American had to put down a new ball every second hole or so, because so much damage was done to the ball-covers by his "scored" clubs.

It was in the same year that the Rules of Golf Committee banned the use of "corrugated, grooved or slotted" clubs. While regarding these as involving a substantial departure from rule, the Committee did not consider that patterns scored or punched on the faces of iron clubs "in a manner customary for a number of years" could be held to be a substantial departure. But it was added that anyone in doubt about the legality of a particular club could forward it to St. Andrews for a ruling.

This injunction was not completely effective, for two years later, at Troon, just before the start of the

Open Championship, an official statement threatened with disqualification any competitor playing with illegal clubs and added:

The Rules of Golf Committee has decided that clubs with corrugated, grooved or slotted patterns . . . are not permissible. . . . Clubs have from time to time been submitted with faces so marked by punches or otherwise as to produce an effect similar to those above described . . . and consequently are not permissible in the Open Championship.

This caused no small commotion among the competitors, both British and American, and the files in the shop of Willie Fernie, the Troon professional, were kept merrily at work on the evening before the championship began.

I was reminded of that occurrence a quarter of a century later when, during the Ryder Cup match at Ganton, Ben Hogan, the U.S. non-playing captain, objected to some of the clubs used by the British team, alleging that they did not conform to regulations.

Great excitement prevailed in the official hotel in Scarborough, with conferences of all kinds, until the offending clubs were sent for adjudication to a distinguished member of the Rules of Golf Committee who was staying some miles out of Scarborough. He examined them and returned them to the officials with the remark that "there is nothing a little filing will not put right."

To go back to the mid-twenties: six months after the Troon *démarche* the U.S.G.A. backed up St. Andrews by going characteristically into more detail on the subject. It was stipulated that club faces should not bear

any lines, dots, or other markings made for the obvious purpose of putting a cut on the ball, nor shall they be stamped or cut with lines exceeding 1/16th of an inch in width nor less than 3/32nds of an inch apart, measured from their inside edges. Both dot and line markings may be used either alone or in combination with the above limitations, provided all raised or rough edges are removed.

In 1931 the R. & A. felt impelled to state that attention had been given to "certain clubs with striking faces having a concavity much more pronounced than those hitherto in use." They were declared illegal, and in the United States sand-wedges with concave faces were also barred.

Later the U.S.G.A. altered its specification to limit the width of a groove to 1/32 of an inch while retaining the 3/32 space between grooves. This meant that the rules permitted the width of one groove and one space between grooves to total no more than one eighth of an inch. To assist manufacturers the U.S.G.A. drew up a memorandum, but the details of this and the substance of the R. & A. decisions have been incorporated in the present rules.

Up to 1951 the Rules of Golf Committee sanctioned a club with a movable head giving several degrees of loft, designed to allow a player to carry only one club and use it for various shots. This type of club was at that time banned in the United States, and in the 1952 code Britain came into line by agreeing to the insertion of the following paragraph in Rule 2: "A club shall be one unit. All its various parts shall be permanently fixed. No part may be movable or separate or capable of adjustment by the player."

Later this became and still is: "No part of the club may be movable or separable or capable of adjustment during a round of play. The player or other agency shall not change the characteristics of a club during a round."

Since the war, too, there has been legislation on the grip, which may not now have a channel or furrow or be moulded for any part of the hands. Also banned is any device to give the player artificial aid in gripping or swinging the club "even though it be not a part of the club." This clause was inspired, no doubt, by various innovations, one of which was designed to ensure that the arms swung the club, but which would have been very awkward, if not impossible, to use anywhere except on the practice ground.

By rule and decision and appendix there has now developed a formidable amount of legislation on "form and make." It is just another example of over-elaboration of rules due to two main causes—the fact that rule-making is now considered necessary for repressing the dishonest as well as guiding the honest; and the passion of the legal mind for closing every possible loophole and providing for every possible contingency.

Over-simplification can be as dangerous as over-elaboration, and I know the difficulties which would attend any attempt to reduce the present code to more reasonable proportions. The happy mean is never easy to achieve.

But the rules are steadily getting more remote from reality and from the ordinary golfer, because he has neither the patience to study them nor, in many cases, the ability to understand them. This is a question which ought to be considered very carefully by the Rules of Golf Committee, who have a moral duty to make all golfers rules-conscious.

CHAPTER V

On—and Off—the Course

THERE are many points in the development of the rules by which we may trace the evolution of golf courses from the free-ranging links of the seashore in a state of nature to the enclosed spaces designed by man.

The present rule, for example, describes "the course" as the whole area over which play is permitted (Definition 11) and points out that it is the duty of the authorities in charge to define its boundaries accurately. While this definition embraces all ground within the boundaries, it is sub-divided by other definitions into three distinct areas for each hole. They are the teeing-ground, the putting-green, and "through the green," the last meaning the whole of the course except "all hazards and the teeing-ground and the putting-green of the hole being played."

Between the wars the definition of the course was slightly different, reading: ". . . the whole area within which play is permitted; more particularly . . . the ground between the holes which is specially prepared for play." Most golfers still regard this as the case, since "off the course" is a common description of a shot which has landed in the rough. The development from open free-ranging golf to the game played on spaces encircled by private property is the main reason why we now have an Out of Bounds Rule. With no boundaries in existence the wayward golfer might stray far from the straight line with no other penalty than the difficulty of getting into play again. But the enclosure of courses often meant that a shot only slightly off the line might be out of bounds, and it was necessary to exact a penalty for giving the golfer the privilege of a second shot from the orginal spot.

The first mention of "out of bounds" occurs in the code of 1899, which stipulated that if a ball be driven out of bounds "a ball shall be dropped at the spot from which the stroke was played under penalty of the loss of the distance." Later it was provided that a local rule could be made adding a penalty stroke to the score for the hole. This "distance only" rule with the qualification persisted until 1920, when the Rules of Golf provided "stroke and distance" as the penalty and clubs were permitted to remit the penalty stroke by local rule.

Now, under the general injunction that clubs

may not make local rules which waive any penalty under the Rules of Golf, this dispensation is withheld and the "stroke and distance" rule applies in all cases. Many golfers feel the penalty is too harsh, and press for a reduction to "distance only," on the grounds that a full shot which goes out of bounds is a better shot than one which misses the ball altogether and costs distance only. This idea was tried out in the experimental code of 1950–1 and was applied also to lost and unplayable balls. But it proved a failure because the application of "distance only" to an unplayable ball was wide open to abuse.

The difficulty might be overcome by reserving "distance only" as the penalty for balls out of bounds or lost, and limiting a player who deems his lie unplayable to the liberty of dropping a ball behind the unplayable lie under a penalty of two strokes. It would at any rate encourage the golfer to "have a go" and prevent frivolous applications of the unplayable-ball rule.

In the early days of enclosed courses the only out-of-bounds areas were those outside the boundaries of the course. But in recent years there has been a tendency, particularly by golf clubs having easy or ill-designed courses, to make up for deficiencies in severity or design by artifical out-of-bounds areas within the confines of the course. This is done by the cutting of shallow ditches between fairways, using rows of saplings as boundaries, or even by marking white lines as arbitrary boundaries. Sometimes this

On the links of North Berwick, with Bass Rock in the background, are several golfers and caddies whose dress suggests a date about eighty years ago. The caddies by then had caddie-bags, but had not got out of the habit of carrying clubs under the arm. Notice how, even as late as the eighties, putting-greens were far from being the velvety swards we expect today.

Two types of Schenectady Putter. That on the left has an aluminium head. The other head is of wood, and this club is believed to be the actual putter used by Walter J. Travis of the United States in the Amateur Championship at Sandwich in 1904.

"With instruments singularly ill-adapted to the purpose." These odd and unusual (and most illegal) clubs, on display in the U.S.G.A. Museum, seem to fit the quotation.

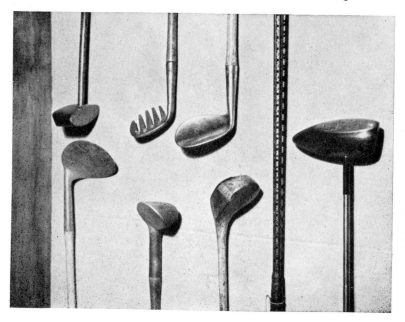

occurs even on first-class courses. On the Royal Liverpool links at Hoylake, for example, a player is out of bounds to the left of a cutting alongside the third fairway, and to the left of the seventh green. At the latter point we have the absurd situation that a ball played from the seventh teeing-ground could finish on the eighth teeing-ground and yet, according to the out-of-bounds rule and the definition of boundaries by the local committee, be "off the course."

The ball out of bounds, like those other abstract forms "lost," "unplayable," and "provisional," deserves sympathy. They are all associated with misfortune, and of the four "provisional" would seem to merit the greatest compassion.

Like the mule, it has no pride of ancestry and almost no hope of posterity. Introduced only in cases where the original ball may have encountered trouble, it is born of despair, is illegitimate from birth, and can gain an honest status only by a metamorphosis which sometimes transforms it into "the ball in play." Since this change usually involves its owner in the loss of two strokes, the last state of the provisional ball is little better than the first. And as it takes a final plunge into the oblivion of the hole for a seven which in happier circumstances might have been a four, it probably reflects in its little rubber-cored mind that nothing can atone for the disgrace of having been born "provisional."

Much more exciting and satisfying are the

adventures of those better-born but wayward types "lost," "out of bounds," and "unplayable." To have endured many ill-timed blows in the heat of the day and then go whizzing into the sanctuary of the rough, lying coyly and snugly under autumn leaves while caddies, players, and spectators shuffle around in a fruitless search, suits the impish nature of the "lost" ball. It is pleasant to rest after the syncopated progress from teeing-ground to green and listen to the searchers walking to and fro over the hiding-place, turning over every leaf but the right one, and giving vent at intervals to such remarks as "It couldn't have been as far as this"; "I hit it rather well"; "It wouldn't run far in this stuff"; "These leaves are a damn nuisance," etc.

And finally come the welcome words: "All right, chaps, let's get on," and the noise of pursuit dies away. Sooner or later, of course, "lost" becomes "found" and will be picked up by a total stranger looking for something else. But there will have been the respite from hard play and still pleasant uncertainty as to the future. When one's fate can range from being thrown to the dog or put into the practice bag of a champion, it cannot be said that life lacks variety. A rest of some duration is also the lot of "unplayable," although not until after adventure fraught with danger. To cannon off a tree-trunk into the prickly interior of a gorse-bush may be a painful process, but it is followed by the knowledge that there is safety from the savage edge of a niblick or the bludgeoning of the blaster.

To dive into a rabbit-hole may be a shock, but there is compensation in the realization that no golf club legal at St. Andrews can be used in such circumstances.

Yes, to be unplayable is almost as comfortable as being lost, but from the point of view of uncertainty and variety there is nothing to beat the state of being out of bounds. Once off the course a ball never knows what fate awaits it. If it lands gently on the other side of a fence bearing a notice "Balls hit over this fence are not recoverable," it can look forward to a fairly long rest. At the worst, it will be collected by the owner of the property and disposed of. At the best, it will lie luxuriously in lush grass and decay slowly and painlessly into a tangled mass of perished rubber, forgotten by man and immune from punishment by man-made clubs.

On the other hand, it may bound into someone's garden, there (O Horror!) to be seized and mangled by the dog, or (O Heaven!) be collected with glee by children and putted gently over a soft lawn.

The lost ball is mentioned in the earliest rules of golf, not surprisingly since on the courses of the eighteenth century and with the imperfect poor-flying "featheries" there could have been nothing easier and certainly nothing more expensive than to lose a ball. So the 1744 code stated with feeling: "If

75

you should lose your ball by its being taken up or any other way, you are to go back to the spot where you struck last and drop another ball and allow your adversary a stroke for the misfortune."

This is substantially the case now, but in between there have been several variations. The lost ball has always been a vexing question for golfers, partly because of the frustration involved and partly because no one likes to waste time and energy in walking back to play another ball. There are many occasions in friendly matches when the player whose ball is lost is allowed to drop another somewhere near the spot and play on under an agreed penalty. I have encountered many cases of golfers really believing they are entitled to do so under the rules. It is of course incorrect, and for a very good reason. The stipulated round in a stroke competition must be played, and this applies also to each hole played out in a match. And, although it is possible to drop a ball behind an unplayable lie and still play the stipulated round, it is impossible to drop behind a lie which is unknown, as in the case of a ball which cannot be found.

Despite the common sense of this argument, it must be recorded that for a long time, nearly seventy years in fact, and within the control of the Honourable Company, there existed a rule which allowed a ball to be dropped under a penalty of one stroke "as near as can be judged to where the original ball was lost."

This was not only much easier than the "stroke and distance" rule introduced by the Edinburgh golfers in 1744, but it also departed from the principle of playing the stipulated round. Yet the experiment was long-lived, lasting from 1775 until 1839, when the Honourable Company returned to the original rule. In 1888 when a really "universal" code was introduced, it included the well-known "lost ball lost hole" clause, which lasted for thirty-two years and became so much a part of the game that even now there are golfers who believe it to be still in force.

It applied only to match-play, of course, and read: "In match-play a ball lost entails the loss of the hole. Should a ball not be found within ten minutes the opposite side can claim the hole."

Obviously some provision had to be made for continuity in stroke-play, so the "Special Rules for Medal-Play" adopted the stroke-and-distance rule of previous codes with an important variation. The stroke rule read: "If a ball be lost the player returns to the spot as near as possible to where the ball was struck, tees another ball and loses a stroke. If the lost ball be found before he has struck the other ball, the first ball shall continue the one to be played." This meant that the ball put into play could be teed, even if the ball lost had not been struck from a teeing-ground.

Three years after the introduction of these new rules the time allowed for search was reduced to five

minutes and remains so to this day. It should be
noted that in the 1899 code, where a "distance only"
rule was introduced for a ball driven out of bounds,
the penalty for a lost ball remained stroke and
distance.

The provisional-ball rule has considerably eased
the troubles involved in losing balls. If the original
ball has gone out of sight into country where it might
be lost, the golfer can play another ball which
becomes the ball in play if the original cannot be
found.

There has also been misunderstanding among
golfers as to the exact implications of the "five
minutes" clause. It is clear, however, from Decision
56/34/10 that, although a player can declare the ball
lost at any time before the expiry of five minutes, he
is entitled to play the ball if found within five minutes provided he has not put another ball into play
or played any provisional ball beyond the point of
loss. This is probably the only situation in golf where
a player is allowed to change his mind and get away
with it.

In recent years there has been a change in the
official mind concerning the exasperating situation of
a player holing out, being unaware of the fact, and
giving up his ball as lost. In 1910 a decision was
given that the player in this position must be held to
have lost the hole. The latest decision (52/20)
concerned a player in a stroke competition who holed

out with his tee-shot but did not know this, went
back to the tee, played another ball, and holed out
with that in three strokes. Only then did he discover
his first ball in the hole. It was ruled that his score
with the first ball counted. An earlier decision to the
same effect made the point that a ball holed is an
incontrovertible fact and that no player could be
penalized for what happened after the ball had been
holed out.

The unplayable-ball rule in its present form is
the fruit of more than a century of endeavour to deal
adequately with the undeniable fact that on some
occasions the ball just cannot be played as it lies.

Our ancestors of the eighteenth century were
uncompromising. It was considered an unwritten
law that the ball had to be played as it lay or the
hole surrendered. And this served well so long as golf
was played exclusively by matches. But the introduction of stroke-play created problems which could
not be solved so easily.

In 1775 the ball had to be played "where it
lyes," and this principle was maintained in subsequent codes until in 1858 it was ordained that in
match-play the ball must be played or the hole
given up, and in stroke-play the golfer could lift the
ball from anywhere on the course under a penalty of
two strokes.

Some years earlier, in 1851, an ingenious experiment had been tried by the introduction of a rule

which allowed the opponent to protest against the ball being lifted but obliged him to support his claim by proving the ball playable.

If the opponent thought the ball playable, he could strike at it and, if getting it clear in two strokes, could then oblige the owner of the ball to carry on playing it with those two strokes added to the owner's score for the hole. If, however, the opponent failed to make the ball playable in two strokes, the player was at liberty to lift and drop under penalty, as if the trial had never been made.

So unwieldy a rule must have been difficult to apply and, in any case, almost impossibly ambiguous. Who, for example, was to say whether the ball was playable or not after the two trial strokes? In 1852 the rule was amended to the extent that the opponent was required not to remove it from the unplayable lie, but merely to make it playable—although no guidance was given as to how one could assess the "playability" of the lie. Presumably if the ball lay in a cart rut, for instance, and the opponent delivered a blow which removed the earth ridge without moving the ball, he might be said to have made the ball "playable." The second version was no better than the first, but it must have worked, for it lasted five more years. That fact is not more remarkable than that it was ever introduced.

The rule of 1858 prescribing loss of hole in a match or two strokes in a competition lasted until 1920, when the present stroke-and-distance rule was introduced and applied to both match-play and stroke-play. In the latter case, however, the golfer had the alternative of teeing a ball behind the unplayable lie under a penalty of two strokes.

Today, of course, the alternative applies to both forms of golf, the player in match- or medal-play having the choice of going back under "stroke and distance" or dropping a ball behind or near to the unplayable lie under a penalty of two strokes. It should be noted that "teeing-up" is no longer allowed. A player can drop as far behind the lie as he pleases, so long as he keeps the original spot between him and the hole; but if this be impossible because of the topography, he must drop as near as possible to the lie and not nearer the hole.

Now we come to a short period during which the old inexorable "play the ball as it lies" regime and the less austere "stroke and distance" rule were both abandoned in the general attempt to make conditions more acceptable to the average golfer. The experimental code of 1950–1 reduced the penalty in the case of an unplayable ball to "distance only," with the alternative of dropping two club-lengths behind the lie with a penalty of one stroke. The provisional ball no longer applied in this case, and the reasons for this will be dealt with more fully later, but the effect of the experimental reduction in penalties, even with the provisional ball prohibited, was to make it far too easy for the golfer to extricate himself from the consequences of a bad stroke. The whole trouble was that the rules allowed the player to be the sole judge of whether his lie was playable or not.

Under the pre-1950 rule no golfer, whether he lost stroke and distance or two strokes, would invoke the unplayable-ball clause if he thought he had a chance of doing better by playing the ball as it lay. The balance, if anything, was in favour of his making the attempt if there was a good chance of getting clear in two strokes and even a remote possibility of becoming playable in one stroke.

But the 1950 rule meant that in the majority of situations it was no longer worth while "having a go." To lose distance or one stroke, according to which alternative was adopted, was usually a far better proposition than playing the ball as it lay and risking failure. So golfers everywhere adopted a cynical attitude towards one of the fundamental principles of golf. The player was the sole judge of his lie, the rules allowed a simple way out of difficulties which might prove costly, and it would be foolish not to take advantage of the fact. During the golf seasons of 1950 and 1951 there were many incidents illustrating this point. The most celebrated one, because it had a bearing on the leading places in the Open Championship, concerned an overseas competitor who was bunkered at the short thirteenth on Troon Old Course. The ball lay badly in the bunker, but was not unplayable, although it was possible that even a good stroke might not achieve complete recovery. The player declared the ball unplayable, played another tee-shot which finished near to the pin, and holed the putt for a three, counting the first tee-shot.

Shortly afterwards a British player finished in the same bunker. He took two shots to get out and the hole cost him five. One might adopt a very high moral attitude and say one player exploited the letter of the law and the other was true to the spirit. But it was the law which provided the loophole, and this basic weakness of the experimental rule was made so clear that at the end of the period there was general agreement that the law must be made more severe.

Unfortunately, in restoring the stroke-and-distance or two-strokes penalty for the unplayable ball the revisionists made this apply also to a ball out of bounds—a step which many golfers at the time felt to be unnecessary.

I think this point worthy of consideration. Take the case of two players in a stroke competition. Player A pushes out his drive into some bushes near a boundary fence. Player B pushes out his drive also, but, hitting slightly the longer ball, sees it finish out of bounds. Player B has no option but to drive again, counting three strokes. But Player A, whose first shot was no better than the other, has the chance of recovery to a position where he is as well off in two strokes as the other golfer is in three.

Stroke and distance or the equivalent penalty of dropping behind under two strokes is necessary for an unplayable ball to avoid abuse. And the stroke-

and-distance penalty should also apply to a lost ball to guard against deliberate failure to find a ball. But a ball out of bounds is a fact, and on most courses a contingency more frequent than either of the others.

So far as the unplayable ball was concerned, the reversion to the old penalties was justified, and it made possible the reintroduction of the "provisional ball" rule which in one form or another had been part of the game for something like sixty years. In 1899 the first out-of-bounds rule was introduced, allowing the dropping of a ball, under loss of distance only, at the spot from which the last stroke had been played. In 1902 the following paragraph was added: "If it be doubtful whether a ball has been played out of bounds, another may be dropped and played, but if it be discovered that the first ball is not out of bounds it shall continue in play without penalty." In 1920 the rule was extended to cover lost or unplayable balls, and dignified by the official intimation that it had been introduced "to save delay."

During the next few years there were many criticisms of the provisional-ball rule, and in the preamble to the 1928 Official Decisions, No. 2 stated:

The Rules of Golf Committee is aware that in the case of an unplayable ball, under certain exceptional circumstances, a stricter law, which would enact that a player could only go back to play his next stroke after determining the position of his ball from the previous stroke, would provide more exact justice.

The Rules of Golf Committee consider, however, that

in practice the provisional ball clauses have successfully fulfilled their purpose of "saving delay" without interfering with the proper regulation of the game.

So the provisional ball is now firmly established as a legal device to save time, although it must be admitted there are certain objections to it on the ground of possible abuse, particularly when, as the rules allow, a golfer plays a second provisional ball, or even a third, and there is no means of checking the truth of his statement if he declares that the ball he finds is his original ball, when it might well be one of the other balls played.

In these days of crowded courses it is nevertheless very convenient to be able to avoid walks back along the course with the increase in congestion entailed.

CHAPTER VI

The Starting-Point

ALTHOUGH sub-editors and others who deal with my writings no doubt regard me as an old pedant, I like to stick to the phrase "teeing-ground" when referring to the starting-place for each hole. This is now commonly called the "tee," but that word refers not to the ground but to the eminence on which the ball is perched for the first stroke.

Golfers who began play less than thirty years ago will describe that eminence as a "tee-peg," and perhaps it is natural for them to regard the ground in which the tee-peg is placed as the "tee." Their elders, however, could recall the days when the tee was of sand, either a shapeless mound on which the ball sat like a miniature moon in the crater of a miniature Vesuvius (when we manufactured it ourselves) or a neat cone made with a pinch of sand (when the caddie did the job).

Those were the days when caddies, for comparatively modest fees, performed such humble tasks as making the tee and cleaning all the clubs with emery paper during and after the round. Without a caddie the player would take a handful of sand from the tee-box (now used as a receptacle for cigarette cartons and ball-wrappers), slap it on the turf, and painfully erect a mountain. The player with a caddie, on the other hand, would take his stance, select a spot for the ball, tap on the turf with his driver-head, say "High" or "Low," and leave the caddie to do the rest.

For some time after tee-pegs became popular many golfers continued this practice, but it soon fell into disuse, partly because the use of the peg was simple and allowed the player to get just the height he wanted, and partly because the character of the caddie and his attitude to golfers and manual labour underwent changes for the worse. By that time caddies had been emancipated by rustless finishes from the hard labour of cleaning, and had developed democratic ideas about the indignity of teeing-up for an employer who was quite capable of doing the job himself and, in any case, would improve his waist-line by doing so.

This point was made clear to George Duncan, then the Open Champion, during his American tour of 1920. On a course in the Southern states, before starting a match, he was allotted a huge, cheerful Negro, who watched with great interest while Dun-

can selected a spot, tapped it, and waited for the
teeing-up process to begin. Nothing happened, so
Duncan tapped again and said: "I'll have it there,
caddie."

Then the Negro looked at Duncan, eyes rolling
sympathetically, and asked: "What's the matter,
mistah? You got lumbago?"

My preference for calling the teeing-place a
"teeing-ground" and the tee-peg a "tee" is based not
on fancy but on traditional fact. In the earliest code,
the 1744 code of the Gentlemen Golfers, Rule 2
reads: "Your tee must be upon the ground." It seems
strange that in a code of only thirteen rules and 339
words (as against something like 25,000 words
today) there should have been this insistence on an
apparently small point when so many more important
contingencies were not mentioned. Since the teeing-
ground of those days was no bigger than a millwheel
—it was, in fact, the ground within a club-length of
the hole—there could have been no other place for a
sand tee than "on the ground." Were there in those
days some bright sparks who tried to perch the ball
on the end of a stick, thinking thereby to gain some
advantage of distance? A forerunner, perhaps, of Sir
Harold (then Mr.) Gillies, who in 1924 (in the
Amateur Championship, of all events, and at St.
Andrews, of all places) used a tee constructed from
a beer-bottle supporting a length of rubber tubing
on the end of which the ball was placed, and from

which it was dispatched with a driver having what in those days was a very large deep-faced head.

It caused a lot of amusement, provided the photographers with pictures and the press with "copy," and Sir Harold himself with a lot of puckish humour over the reactions of outraged authority. While the inventor of the "bottle tee" was enjoying himself on the Old Course, the following solemn notice was posted for the information of competitors, the press, and (doubtless) Mr. Gillies himself:

The Rules of Golf Committee hopes that golfers, before making use of abnormal methods of play, or abnormal implements, will earnestly consider whether they are acting in conformity with the spirit of the Rules of Golf, and in particular with the spirit of the regulations governing the Form and Make of golf clubs. The Committee considers that it is much to be deplored that players, instead of trying to master the use of golf clubs, should endeavour to overcome the difficulties of the game by using implements which have never been associated with it.

One may ask whether all that pompous verbiage was necessary to deal with a situation which could have been handled much better by a good hearty gust of laughter at the Gillies contraption and a short sharp injunction to that distinguished surgeon to "cut it out." In fact, Gillies said as much when he read the notice, and other comments of the day no doubt made everyone concerned anxious to forget the whole thing as soon as possible. It may be noted that neither then nor at any subsequent time did the Committee legislate against a recurrence of attempts to introduce "abnormal" tees. The 1934 rules (Definition 16) stated that in teeing "the ball may be placed on the ground or on sand or other substance in order to raise it off the ground," and the same wording is in use today.

Theoretically, since there is nothing in the rules to limit the meaning of "other substance" or any limit as to the height of the tee, there is nothing to prevent another leg-pull by another Gillies.

Whatever the reason for Rule 2 in the 1744 code, it did indicate that the practice of making a tee had been common for some time. In the very early days when the ground played over was rough and indistinguishable from the surrounding countryside it would have been natural for players, when starting, to agree on placing the ball instead of throwing it on to the ground with the risk of finding a bad lie. And the golfer allowed to place his ball would be just human if, in placing, he took advantage of any hump in the ground which would elevate his ball and make the first stroke as easy as possible.

Earliest definition of a teeing-ground, as I have already indicated, was in Rule 1 of the 1744 code— "You must tee your ball within a club's length of the hole." This, to the present-day golfer accustomed to vast expanses of beautifully mown turf, must sound almost incredible, but the putting-greens in the eighteenth century were merely small patches of ground cropped by rabbits and in later years scythed by those responsible for "keeping the green."

In such circumstances, if a greater degree of latitude for teeing had been permitted, disputes must have occurred between golfers choosing good spots or contesting the choice of their opponents. So it became the custom to take sand from the hole after holing out and tee-up alongside for the next drive.

The system at least had the advantage, almost unknown today, of avoiding walks between putting-green and teeing-ground.

In 1777, doubtless from a desire to protect the vicinity of the hole from the schlaffs of driver-heads and the ruins of sand-tees, the teeing-ground was described as "not nearer than one club-length nor further than four club-lengths" from the hole. In 1828 the minimum was two and the maximum still four, altered in 1859 to six and eight. By this time the putting-green was becoming distinct from the teeing-ground, and after 1875, when the "teeing-ground" is mentioned for the first time and defined as "between eight and twelve club-lengths from the hole," separate teeing-grounds became customary. It was not until 1893 that the exact shape and dimensions of the area were laid down. It was defined as the space between the markers to a depth of two club-lengths, and has remained so ever since.

Once the limits were defined, there had to be a

penalty for teeing-up outside those limits. In a match a player driving from outside was liable to have his stroke recalled by the opponent, and still is, but in 1899 a new rule for stroke-play imposed disqualification as the penalty. That rather harsh rule has been watered down to the extent that now a player infringing it must count his stroke so played and then drive again from within the proper limits. Only if he fails to do this and carries on with the ball driven illegally is he disqualified, very properly, for not having played the stipulated course.

Having decided the limits, golfers had to decide on the order of starting, and this was not provided for in the earliest rules, no doubt because it was a comparatively unimportant point which could be decided on by drawing lots. On the other hand, I am inclined to believe that what is now called the "honour," or the "privilege," of playing first must have derived from the days when the game was played mainly by nobles or wealthy personages, and in matches due deference would probably be paid to the higher-ranking player or players by inviting him or them to do their opponents "the honour" of driving first. When James II as Duke of York took as his partner an Edinburgh shoemaker named John Patersone to play a money match against two English noblemen, there can be no question that His Royal Highness was invited to take "the honour."

This tradition is perpetuated in the current practice at most golf clubs of allowing the Captain's match to start at his pleasure, no matter what other matches are waiting to play. But as a general rule nowadays the honour is determined by more democratic means. In the case of a competition the player whose name appears first on the draw drives first. In friendly matches the honour is taken by the player with the lowest handicap, and in more serious encounters the toss of a coin may decide. There is no mention in the 1744 code of precedence on the teeing-ground, although it does include a rule of procedure still in force, that the party farthest from the hole plays first.

Earliest reference to order of striking from the tee occurs in the Aberdeen Golf Club's code of 1783 —"The party gaining a hole shall have the privilege of striking off first as long as the opposite party do not make good a hole." In the St. Andrews code dated 1857 it is stated: "The person entitled to play off first shall be named by the parties concerned; and although the courtesy of starting is generally granted to old captains of the club or members, it may be settled by lot or toss of a coin—the party gaining the hole is to lead."

Later, in the 1882 revised code, Rule 4 states: "The side gaining a hole shall lead at the next. . . . This privilege is called 'The Honour.'"

In the light of later experience it may be asked whether on this matter tradition has not been followed too closely, with the result that what was at first regarded as a privilege can very often be a dis-

93

advantage. Two hundred years ago, when courses were as rough as nature made them and modern accuracy in stroke-play impossible, the "honour" rule was a convenient means of controlling the order of play. But nowadays tactics and strategy play a much greater part in the game, aided by the use of accurate standardized equipment, and many golfers are of the opinion that the honour should convey not the privilege of playing first, but the right to choose which side shall do so. There are many occasions when it would be an advantage to have the opponents play first. Sometimes a bad shot by the opponent would make it possible to play safe at a difficult hole. Often it is useful to watch the result of the opponent's stroke at some short hole and then choose club and method accordingly. And there must also be many occasions when a climb to a high teeing-ground or a long walk places the holder of the honour at a physical disadvantage, since he must tee-up immediately and his opponent has time to recover breath and poise. It would be a useful experiment by the Rules of Golf Committee to revise this rule so that the player winning a hole would have the option of driving first from the next teeing-ground or requiring his opponent to do so, on condition that the order of play should alternate at succeeding holes until another hole changes hands.

Except for insistence on the honour and the order of play through the green, the early rules allowed players to get off the mark unembarrassed by a great number of Dos and Don'ts. But, as with other rules, the march of progress meant elaboration as successive law-makers strove to close loopholes and answer the problems of experience. So eventually there was provision for most contingencies. The case of a ball falling off a tee while being addressed had to have a rule to itself. Then there came injunctions about playing the ball as it lay, improving lie or stance, moving loose impediments. There was a rule to forbid striking the ball unfairly and another showing how it should be dropped or placed when the rules allowed this to be done. It was also necessary to say when you could or could not lift the ball, and protocol for dealing with a ball interfering with play was extended to four paragraphs.

It has often been said that the rules developed from a short code for honest men to a complete legislation for dealing with deliberate evasion, and this chapter concludes with the account of a curious example of the fact that many modern golfers cannot be trusted to play the game fairly. It concerned a decision given some forty years ago about the order of play in a foursome. Prior to 1875, although it was accepted that players in foursomes should play in turn, there was no penalty for playing out of turn. But in that year was introduced the following rule: "If in a doubles match a person shall play twice in succession he loses the hole." That rule holds good today, with the addition of a penalty of two strokes in a stroke competition or disqualification if the side fail to put a ball in play at the spot from which the first incorrect stroke was made.

In the case I have mentioned, a woman player in a mixed foursome thought she would be unable to carry a ravine running across the course. Her partner, as he afterwards admitted, told her to miss the ball completely and then made a stroke himself, landing the ball on the green.

It was ruled that, since there was no intention on the woman's part to strike or move the ball, the movement she made with the club could not be called a stroke. Therefore her partner played out of turn, and since they failed to rectify that error by putting another ball in play, they were disqualified for not playing the stipulated round.

CHAPTER VII

Playing Fair

THE tendency during the nineteenth century towards more complex rules was a clear indication that the spread of the game had produced a golf population less well-schooled in the art of "doing the right thing." And, as usual, there arose the necessity for making sure that everyone everywhere did the same things in the same way.

Regimentation might not be so pleasant as the free-and-easy ways of earlier days, but it was essential to keep control of the game by ensuring that, so far as possible, every likely contingency was provided for in the rules.

It would be wrong to suggest that our golfing ancestors were paragons of virtue on the links. Indeed, when courses were so rough as to be nine parts hazards there were many more opportunities than now for a golfer to gain some illicit advantage, and these were no doubt exploited by shady charac-

97

ters or even by honest men in the excitement of playing for a big wager.

But golf in those days was almost exclusively by matches generally played between mutual friends and acquaintances who knew each other's weaknesses as well as each other's strengths, and arranged the matches accordingly.

Now, with courses kempt and hazards few in number and clearly defined, the situation demands rules to cover all kinds of intentional and unintentional acts which might improve a golfer's chance of saving a stroke. And there must also be provision for regular procedure in the case of certain difficulties.

These are covered mainly by Rules 16 to 24, of which Rule 21, relating to the "wrong ball," is dealt with elsewhere. The first of these rules is the modern version of the basic principle that the ball must be played as it lies; but a version robbed of much of its old-time severity.

"The ball," it reads, "shall not be touched or moved purposely and must be played as it lies (except as otherwise provided for in the Rules or Local Rules)."

Some of these rules are penal, as, for instance, the injunction in Rule 17 against improving one's lie in the rough or moving or breaking growing things to facilitate the execution of a stroke. Others are directional, like Rule 22 prescribing the proper method of dropping or placing a ball lifted in play.

Rule 17 was introduced in 1888 as a ban on pressing down inequalities of surface or moving, bending, or breaking anything growing. Three years later this was qualified by adding: "except in taking the stance or in soling the club."

In the modern code there is a further qualification: "The club may be grounded only lightly and must not be pressed on the ground."

This was quoted by the United States Golf Association some years ago when dealing with the case of a player whose ball landed in a heel-mark in loose sand which was not a hazard. Grounding his club at the address, as he was entitled to do, the player began his backswing by drawing the club along the sand, thus clearing a path for the downswing and virtually removing the difficulty of the heel-mark.

It was ruled that the player lost the hole for improving the lie of the ball.

In 1911 a player at Worlebury picked up a flat stone and stood on it to play a stroke. The Rules of Golf Committee of that day, admitting there was no rule to cover the point, declared that "by the custom of the game the player is not permitted to build a stance."

Not until twenty-three years later was this decision incorporated in the rules, and the affair is an interesting illustration of how, despite the reluctance of the authorities, the rules were steadily becoming more complex and more voluminous as golfers became more ignorant of the "customs of the game" or more negligent in observing them.

It is important to remember, in connection with this "stance" rule, that, while a golfer is not permitted to build a stance, he cannot be prevented from taking his stance fairly. It has been ruled that a golfer standing on a slippery slope in bad weather was entitled to dig his heels into the soft turf in order to obtain a firm stance.

For the first half of this century the stroke rules allowed a ball to be lifted from any place on the course, the player having the option of losing stroke and distance or teeing-up under a penalty of two strokes behind the spot from which the ball had been lifted. That rule has now given place to the unplayable-ball rule, which, although applying the same penalties, does not allow teeing-up and implies that the ball may be lifted only if the player deems it unplayable.

It is true that the decision of that point is left solely to the player and that a ball may be declared unplayable anywhere on the course, but the moral obligation to keep to the spirit of the rules is quite clear.

Under the old rules there was a decision in 1912 about a player who started a winter round with a white ball but, overtaken by a snowstorm during the play of a hole, lifted the white ball and replaced it by one painted red. He was disqualified for lifting a ball in play and not penalizing himself two strokes.

Presumably that penalty could apply today unless the player declared the white ball unplayable. Or could he change it as being "unfit for play"?

Over the years there has always been a certain amount of doubt about the procedure in dropping a ball when lifted under the rules (Rule 22). Two hundred years ago the procedure was perfunctory in the extreme. If the ball "come among water or any watery filth," the golfer was instructed to throw the ball behind the hazard "six yards at least."

How literally the "six yards at least" was to be applied it is impossible to say. A good thrower might achieve a much greater distance than that and still presumably be within the law. On the other hand, was he to be penalized if the ball, lobbed weakly, stopped only five yards behind the spot?

In 1812, when the first "dropping" rule was introduced, the player had to "front the hole to which he is playing," stand close behind the hazard, and drop the ball behind him "from his head."

The 1858 rules required the player to stand "close on" the hazard, but in 1891 he was allowed to stand "as far as he may please" behind the hazard.

The modern method of dropping over the shoulder was introduced in 1908. Soon afterwards a golfer carrying out this procedure managed to drop the ball into the golf bag hanging from his shoulder.

"Must I play out of the bag," he asked, "or do I treat the ball as lodging in something moving?"

The Rules of Golf Committee has a good answer

to that one. The ball, not having reached the ground, was "not in play," and must be dropped again.

At first glance, Rule 19, which insists that the ball must be fairly struck at with the head of the club, might seem to be legislation against a remote contingency. But there are many situations in golf where a clean stroke is virtually impossible. If the ball lies against a fence or in the middle of a gorse bush, there will always be the temptation to get it out of trouble by hook or by crook. A less usual incident concerned the player who was stymied and lofted his ball over the intervening one by laying his niblick along the turf and drawing it smartly forward, thus getting the effect of loft without making a "fair stroke" at the ball. That idea was very properly stamped on.

Generally speaking, the rules dealt with in this chapter are designed to control both the involuntary peccadillo, committed under the stress of the moment, and the deliberate evasion of the player who is out to win at any cost.

If golfers play fair, they need not fear the rules. But when we consider how many ways a golfer can cheat if he has a mind to it, we ought to be thankful that these and other rules exist to hold him in check.

CHAPTER VIII

Things on the Move

MUCH of what happens to the golf ball in play is the player's fault, although sometimes he is an innocent victim of mischance. But, whether sinned against or sinning, the golfer knows that the majority of the misfortunes befalling him through the green are provided for in that section of the rules which we can call "Trouble Corner." The teeing-ground gives him the best possible start, and once on the putting-green he may reasonably expect to have a clear line to the hole. But in between a thousand and one forces are at work to frustrate him or punish him.

In the first place there is that mysterious and mischievous manifestation known as "an agency outside the match," whose field of activity is controlled by Rules 26 (Ball in Motion Stopped or Deflected) and 27 (Ball at Rest Moved). They are designed to extricate the golfer from the consequences of events outside his control. Between these two rules is an important difference. If a ball in motion is interfered with by an outside agency, it must be played where it comes to rest after the interference. If a ball at rest be displaced, it must be restored to its original position by dropping or placing. There are exceptions to both procedures, but the underlying principle is to minimize the damage a golfer might suffer for an occurrence which is not the result of his own bad play or inadvertent actions. Since it is impossible to say where a moving ball would have finished if it had not been stopped or deflected, the only possible solution must be to play it from where it has come to rest. If it finishes in a bunker, the golfer is unlucky. If it finishes in the bottom of the hole, the golfer is lucky. But in equity no other procedure is possible or fair.

This particular rule has an ancient origin, for the stopping or deflecting of a ball in motion is described in Definition 27 as "a rub of the green," and that phrase is nearly 150 years old. The first known code of written rules included the provision that "if a ball be stopped by any person, horse, dog, or anything else the ball so stopped must be played where it lies."

Thirty-one years later, in 1775, a similar rule had this addition: "But if stopped by the adversary, his Cady or servant, the party who stops the ball to lose one." This delightfully vague proposition gave place in the Royal and Ancient code of 1812 to the following: "Whatever happens to a ball by accident must be reckoned a rub of the green; if, however, the player's ball strike his adversary or his Cady the adversary loses the hole. If it strikes his own Cady the player loses the hole."

Having played for many years under these and similarly ambiguous laws, golfers in 1857 were presented with a rule which covered almost every contingency. Headed "Rubs of the Green," it runs:

Whatever happens to a ball by accident, such as striking any person, or touched with the foot by a third party or by the fore-caddie, must be reckoned a rub of the green and submitted to. If, however, the player's ball strike his adversary or his adversary's caddie or clubs, the adversary loses the hole; or if it strikes himself or his partner or their caddies or clubs, or if he strikes the ball a second time in playing it, the player loses the hole. If the player touch the ball with his foot or any part of his body or with anything except his club, or with his club move the ball in preparing to strike, he loses a stroke; and if one party strikes his adversary's ball with his club, foot, or otherwise, that party loses the hole. But if he plays it inadvertently, thinking it his own, and the adversary also plays the wrong ball, it is then too late to claim the penalty and the hole must be played out with the balls thus changed. If, however, the mistake occurs from wrong information given by one party to the other the penalty cannot be claimed, and the mistake, if discovered before the other party has played, must be rectified by replacing the ball as nearly as possible where it lay. If the player's ball be played away by mistake, or lifted by a third party, then the player must drop a ball as near the spot as possible without any penalty. Whatever happens to a ball on a Medal Day such as a player striking his caddie or himself or his clubs, or moving the ball with the foot, club, or his caddie doing so, or striking it twice before it stops moving, the player in such cases shall lose one stroke only as the Penalty.

The rule-makers of 1857, it will be noted, included under this head several events which are certainly not rubs of the green. Such contingencies as the player moving his ball at the address, or having his ball moved by the opponent, or playing the wrong ball are now covered by different rules, but it was not until 1891 that the ball in motion and the ball at rest were covered by separate rules.

So far as something happening to a ball in flight is concerned, it is "a rub of the green and must be submitted to." A ball in flight is an airy spirit, proceeding from a definite place to a destination unknown, and whatever happens to it before it comes to rest is all in the game. A ball hooked towards a wood strikes a tree and rebounds on to the fairway, or another ball, driven straight down the middle, hits the tractor of a greenkeeper and bounds into a bunker. In neither case is it possible to say where the ball would have finished if not deflected, and the player is obliged to play it as it lies. Rule 26, however, has two exceptions. If the outside agency is a moving object and the ball lodges in it, the ball, or another ball, is to be dropped (or placed) as near as possible to the spot where the object was when the ball lodged in it. And in stroke competitions, while a ball must be played as it lies after being deflected by a competitor, his partner, their caddies or equipment, it is dropped (or placed) if it lodge in the clothing or anything else belonging to the competitor or his side. The reason for both exceptions is that in each case the spot where the ball came to rest on landing in the outside agency or the clothes can be pinpointed with sufficient accuracy to make the dropping of another ball consistent with fair play for everyone.

In the case of a ball at rest moved by an outside agency (Rule 27), the spot where the ball lay before the occurrence is known, and the ball, or another substituted for it, is dropped or placed on the original spot. Rule 27(1*a*) has a note that if the ball moved is not immediately recoverable, another ball may be substituted. An example of this may be taken from a decision of 1913 concerning the case of a cow trampling on a ball which became embedded in a hoof and was carried some distance before becoming dislodged. It was probably unfit for immediate play, and the decision was that, since the cow was an "agency outside the match," the player should drop "*a* ball" without penalty as near as possible to the spot from which the cow had moved the original ball.

Rule 27, like Rule 26, has certain exceptions, which apply if the ball has been moved by the player or anyone on his side, or has been made to move by any action on their part, such as moving loose impediments near the ball, or addressing it for a stroke. In these cases the ball must be played as it lies in its new position. This applies however small the movement. It has been ruled that a player who placed his putter against the ball while lifting the ball for cleaning purposes and who, in taking up the putter, accidentally moved the ball, lost the hole because he replaced the ball.

Penalties inflicted under Rules 26 and 27 are sometimes additional to other penalties. For instance, a player whose ball, played from near a boundary fence, struck him and then went out of bounds was penalized two strokes under Rule 26 and stroke and distance under Rule 29 (Decision 54/126/23). Another interesting decision (54/14/12) was given in the case of a competitor A who, being asked to remove his ball from B's line, merely moved it to one side. While in that position it was struck by the other ball. It was ruled that A's ball, not being "in play," ranked as part of his equipment, and he lost the hole under Rule 26(2b).

It is necessary now to consider the third "moving ball" rule—Rule 25—which penalizes a player who plays while his ball is moving. This is tied up with Rule 27, which provides penalties for moving or causing a ball to move in the address or during the removal of loose impediments. The penalty under Rule 27 is one stroke, and if a ball moves in this way before a player begins his stroke and he strikes it while it is moving, he is penalized two strokes (or loss of the hole in match-play) in addition to the original penalty stroke (Decision 52/3). If, however, the ball does not begin to move until after the player has begun the stroke or the backward swing for the stroke, the penalty of two strokes does not apply since he is obviously unable to avoid the infringement.

Rule 27 and, indirectly, Rule 25 are governed by Definition No. 3—"a ball is deemed to move if it leave its position and come to rest in any other place." "Any other place" is a factual statement, but has puzzled many golfers. Technically, if a ball rolls to an extent of only a fraction of an inch and does not return to its original position it has come to rest in another place, but the phraseology is a trifle too legal for the ordinary golfer. The early rules levied a penalty for moving a ball inadvertently, but did not define movement. In 1888 it was stated: "A ball is considered to have moved if it leaves its original position in the least degree and stops in another; but if a player touch his ball so as to make it merely oscillate and not leave its original position, it is not considered to have been moved."

This explanatory note was also added to the 1950 rules, but subsequently omitted. It should have been retained because it is easier to describe how a ball has not moved than how it has moved. The whole question is bound up with the fact that many infringements can be detected only by the player. In addressing a ball on the fairway or in the rough or on the putting-green it often happens that a player touches the ball with his club to the extent of making it oscillate, or that pressure on the turf behind the ball causes it to appear to move. In most of these cases only the player himself can know whether the ball did indeed move or "merely oscillate."

An even more abstruse application of this definition is in the case of a ball being trodden on by a player while searching for it. This usually occurs in rough grass, and it might be argued that a ball which descends vertically into the ground is still "in the same place" with regard to the topography of the course. Alternatively, it might be impossible to judge whether a ball so trodden on returned to its original position after the foot had been removed. Any doubts on this point have been cleared up by Decision 56/101/43, which states:

A player is penalized for treading on his ball while searching for it if the ball is moved (Definition 3). Whether the ball is moved or not is a question of fact which must be established by all available evidence. In most cases the player himself will be in the best position to determine whether the ball was moved or not, and considerable weight should be given to his evidence. If a ball is trodden into the ground even by a quarter of an inch, and does not return to its original position, it has *moved.*

Which means, in practice, that everything in the last resort depends on the honesty of the player.

CHAPTER IX

Shots from the Shops

LIKE many other legislative evolutions, the "fourteen clubs" rule owes its origin to the march of science and the craze for automation. It was made twenty years ago to control a cult of over-elaboration, a temporary evil, and has remained in force to the disadvantage of the game. In seeking to prevent the use of many more than fourteen clubs the authorities created an arbitrary limit which many golfers now regard as a minimum as well as a maximum. Which may be good for trade, but is bad for golf.

A century ago no golfer used so many as fourteen clubs because the average "set" was not much more than half that number, and it would not have been easy for the caddie to carry many more than eight or nine clubs under the arm, which was the universal method of transporting them in those days. Even when golf bags became popular the number of clubs was limited by the fact that golfers then were accustomed to playing a great variety of strokes with a few clubs, obtaining variations of length and trajectory by different methods of gripping and swinging the clubs. Thus, during the last years of the guttie ball and even up to the years immediately preceding the First World War, the average set consisted of no more than eight clubs—three woods (driver, brassie, and spoon), four irons, and a putter, although the last-named club was often a putting-cleek which could be employed for iron shots when required.

The irons were of various types, but, whatever the actual lofts favoured by their owners, they were so few in number that golfers had to rely on their skill to achieve half-shots, three-quarter-shots, lofting shots, pitch-and-run shots, running approaches, and all manner of other improvisations.

This was true of the day when the shafts of clubs were made from hickory, when players chose clubs one by one with the care of connoisseurs, and when "sets" of clubs were matched only in the sense that they were all regarded by the owner as fit for the job.

Then came the steel shaft, and all was changed. Steel shafts were legalized by the United States Golf Association in 1926, but three years passed before St. Andrews followed suit. By that time the vogue of matched sets and multiplicity of clubs had swept America, reaching really absurd proportions. It was the cult of "one swing and many clubs," and elderly golfers sneered at the younger generation for "buying shots in the shops."

Not content with matched sets of irons numbered 1 to 10, the trade produced half-sizes, so that the golfer uncertain whether a No. 8 was the right club for a particular approach could select 7½ or 8½ as his judgment indicated.

Before long there were double sets of irons and some golfers carried as many as twenty-five clubs. Caddie-bags grew elephantine in size and caddies staggered under great leather holdalls big enough to have carried the caddies themselves. That is, if the bags had been emptied of the great armoury of clubs, and the balls, spare shoes, waterproof suits, and other gear stowed in their cavernous pockets.

British golf spectators had a sample of this ostentation during the Amateur Championship at Prestwick in 1934, when Lawson Little of the United States won with a bag large by British standards but no larger than those brought by other Americans and hung on the shoulders of British caddies. The latter claimed, and unquestionably earned, extra money for the extra work.

Such a ridiculous trend had to be checked somehow, and the Americans, who had started it all, were the first to call a halt. In 1937, announcing a decision to limit the number of clubs per golfer to fourteen as from January 1, 1938, the U.S.G.A. pointed out that,

113

whereas in earlier days players changed their swings for different shots, now they took a different club and used the same swing.

The multiplicity of clubs tends towards mechanization of the game [said the U.S.G.A. statement]. We have come to the conclusion that limitation of the number of clubs would tend to restore the making of individual shots and increase the skill of the player.

A similar proposition by the Rules of Golf Committee to impose a limit at the same time as the U.S.G.A. action was rejected by members of the R. & A. at the Club's business meeting in May 1937 —one of the few occasions on which proposals by the Committee had failed to get approval. But eighteen months later the Committee tried again, and the limitation to fourteen clubs became operative in Britain on May 1, 1939.

As I have already suggested, the authorities in their efforts to cure a disease created a situation in which a golfer considered himself not properly equipped unless he had fourteen clubs. This was of no benefit to anyone except the trade.

Before the advent of steel shafts and matched sets, golfers had been quite happy with ten or even fewer clubs. But it was now the thing to have four woods and ten irons, some of which would be used rarely, if at all, in any one round.

The No. 1 iron gradually fell from favour, but this merely made room for the newest idea in clubs

114

—the wedge. The diehards might stroll round with their small sets and slim bags and scoff at the youngsters, but the youngsters conformed to fashion and a great deal of the pleasure of golf was destroyed.

Limitation of clubs to ten in number would not be popular in several quarters, but it would benefit the game in two ways. It would increase the premium on skill in stroke-production and improvisation, and therefore restore the balance between the long game and the short game. And by reducing the cost of fitting out a golfer it would attract many more beginners who otherwise would be discouraged by the heavy initial costs.

Perhaps the biggest disadvantage of the original fourteen-club rule, however, was that the penalty of disqualification for accidental breach was far too severe. A golfer could be liable to that penalty for an oversight which could not possibly have given him any advantage.

This was shown clearly during the 1955 Amateur Championship at Royal Lytham and St. Annes, Lancashire, when a competitor who had been using a spare driver on the practice field inadvertently slipped it into his bag. The first hole at Lytham is a one-shotter, and he played an iron from the tee. Only when he came to take his driver on the second tee did he realize his mistake, but, as the rule then stood, there was no alternative to disqualification, even though he had only used two clubs of the fifteen in his bag.

Another case at about the same time concerned a golfer who had been limbering-up before his match with the help of a driver having a weighted head, suitable for exercise but of no earthly use for playing a stroke. But he, too, was disqualified because on leaving the practice ground he forgetfully slipped the weighted club in his bag, and therefore carried one too many.

These incidents and many others led to a belated reform, and in the revised code of 1956 the penalty was changed from disqualification to loss of the hole (in match-play) or two strokes (in stroke-play) for every hole at which a violation of the rule occurred.

Long before this much-needed reform was made it would seem that the Committee were conscious of the fact that the rule as it was first framed could have unduly harsh consequences for accidental violation. Thus it was that in 1950 (Decision 60) a lenient view was taken of the case of a player who, when putting on the first green, discovered two strange clubs in his bag. They had been put there inadvertently by a caddie belonging to the following match. It was ruled that the player could not be disqualified for the accidental action of a caddie other than his own.

In the early days of the rule it was interpreted with severity, but later it was modified by several decisions. One of these early in 1950 (Decision 29) ruled that, although there was no objection to partners in a foursome sharing one caddie-bag, this could be allowed only on condition that neither partner had more than fourteen clubs and that each played with his own clubs during the round.

This meant that if each partner wanted fourteen clubs they would have to carry twenty-eight in the one bag and each be careful to use only those in his own set. Yet there seemed no reason why foursome partners should not share one set of fourteen. The owner of the clubs could gain no advantage and his partner, by using unfamiliar clubs, would, if anything, be at a disadvantage.

The force of this argument was realized by the Rules of Golf Committee, and two years later (Decision 52/30) we find them ruling that foursome partners could share a set of fourteen clubs provided they informed their fellow competitors or opponents of their intention to do so.

Having relaxed the original severity, the Committee went a step further in the following year and decided (Decision 53/–/5) that two players in a stroke competition who agreed to share one bag of clubs did not commit a breach of rule, although "the practice is not to be recommended."

It was also decided that partners in better-ball and fourball matches, as well as in foursomes, could share one set provided the total of clubs did not exceed fourteen.

However much they leaned towards mildness in some aspects of the rule, the authorities have always been rigid in their view that there could be no borrowing of clubs. There are many instances of accidental borrowing from which the offenders could have derived no advantage, such as the very common error of snatching the putter from a partner who has just missed a short putt, and using it to tap in the ball from a few inches.

The official view is that any relaxation of the borrowing clause would open the door to abuse, since it would be possible for a player to use many more than fourteen clubs by the mere device of borrowing. There was an actual case, the subject of Decision 52/29, in which a golfer started play with ten clubs carried by his caddie and wanted to borrow at will from ten clubs carried by his chauffeur, who walked with the match.

St. Andrews was horrified. "The player is in fact commencing the round with twenty clubs carried by two caddies," runs the decision, "and should be disqualified."

So the law made for deliberate evasions of that kind has to apply to innocent offenders like the unfortunate lady who thought she had left her No. 3 iron in the clubhouse and, passing her husband, who was in another match, borrowed his No. 3. Before she had time to use it, she found her "lost" club in her bag.

"Sorry," said stern St. Andrews. "The rule was broken by the mere act of borrowing." They were equally strict with the golfer, charged with borrowing his fellow competitor's putter, who naïvely suggested that as he was carrying only thirteen clubs he had not broken the rule.

Perhaps it was a severity of the no-borrowing interpretation which led to reluctance on the part of golfers to transgress this particular part of the rule. Certainly this could be the only explanation of the extraordinary delusion which caused Peter Thomson, the much-travelled Australian golfer, to lose a vital hole in the match-play championship at Turnberry.

He had been practising near the first teeing-ground and, on being called to start, left his No. 8 iron on the practice ground. He discovered his loss on preparing to approach the first green. A friend ran back, retrieved the club, and offered it to Thomson, but the latter refused it on the ground that he would be penalized for adding to his set during play.

In effect he would have been quite within the law in adding to his set in this way, so long as he did not exceed the total of fourteen and made the addition without delaying play.

Thomson was afraid of being penalized for a seemingly inoffensive act, and it is unfortunate that rule-making has developed in such a way that laws introduced to combat fancied evils often penalize the great mass of golfers for subconscious and rarely harmful acts.

But of few laws can it be said that they do not sometimes bear hardly on the innocent.

CHAPTER X

The Wrong Ball

THE world of golf is full of small white balls which from a short distance seem all alike. Looked at more closely, they are seen to bear numbers, emblems, or coloured dots, and some, belonging to careful golfers, might have in addition the indent of a thumb-nail or the stamp of initials.

But, however they are marked, it is not easy to distinguish one ball from another, even on the fair-way, and the average golfer, instead of making quite certain of ownership before playing, is prone to jump to conclusions based on probabilities. And even when marks are examined for identification purposes, it can happen that two or more balls in use in the same match, or a stray ball outside the match, bear identical markings. So, by human carelessness or force of circumstances, unwitting breaches of the "wrong

How would the modern golfer react to the footprints in this bunker at St. Andrews? With his straw hat firmly in place, the golfer is evidently intending to play out sideways, having concluded that discretion is the better part of valour.

"The ball must be played as it lies or the hole be given up." That was no longer the letter of the law in 1899, but Lieutenant Freddie Tait of the Black Watch—he was killed in South Africa a few months later—is carrying out the spirit. This is his famous water shot with a floater ball from the Alps bunker at Prestwick in the Amateur Championship final of 1899. His opponent and conqueror, John Ball, is standing on the steps.

Nowadays roads are not hazards and the club may be grounded on them. But even that freedom would not have helped this anonymous unfortunate of something like half a century ago, seen playing from "The Road" at the back of the seventeenth green at St Andrews, Scotland

ball" rule frequently occur. The penalties are severe —loss of hole in a match or two strokes in a stroke competition—yet the cases multiply.

Golfers of a hundred years ago or even eighty years ago had no such problem. The feather ball had individual characteristics. Its weight, shape, size, and general behaviour were controlled by various circumstances—the size of the leather segments, the way they were stitched together, the number of feathers used and how they were packed; and the general appearance of the ball would undergo considerable changes very quickly after it was first put into use.

For these reasons, and also because there were comparatively few players and the ball did not fly very far, it was not difficult to identify, and cases of playing the wrong ball were neither numerous nor regarded seriously by the golfers of two centuries ago.

Not until 1839 was there any official reference to playing the wrong ball. Then, in the R. & A. code, under the general heading of "Whatever happens to a ball by accident or is done to it by third parties or by the forecaddie must be regarded as a rub of the green," it was stated that one of these contingencies was "playing at it inadvertently thinking it is his [the player's] own."

For many years afterwards, well into the guttieball era, the golfer's attitude to playing the wrong ball remained unchanged. It was "a rub of the green" and there was no question of any penalty for what was a pure accident.

But in the R. & A. code of 1888 (the first code applicable to golf wherever it was played) it was stated under the heading of "Rubs of the Green and Penalties" (Section IX, Paragraph 30):

> If a player or his caddie strike the opponent's ball in any manner that side loses the hole; but if he plays it inadvertently, thinking it is his own, and the opponent also plays the wrong ball, it is then too late to claim the penalty, and the hole must be played out with the balls thus exchanged.

It is clear that the authorities of those days regarded as serious only the act of playing or moving the opponent's ball, and that the playing of a stray ball outside the match was adequately covered by Paragraph 24 of the same rule: "Whatever happens to a ball by accident . . . must be reckoned a Rub of the Green, and submitted to."

That attitude might be regarded as lax in comparison with present-day practice, but it must be remembered that the incidence of stray balls in those days was very low, the playing of an opponent's ball was all part of the give-and-take of match-play, and stroke-play competitions were still comparatively rare.

But by the early nineties many more people were playing golf, there was a greater need for control over competition play, and, it must be confessed, the old spirit and traditions of the game were becoming adulterated. So it became necessary to provide not only for the ordinary accidents of the links but also for the actions of golfers who, if not downright unscrupulous, had a very loose attitude towards the finer shades of right and wrong.

The contingency of a man finding a ball not his own and playing it as though it were his own had to be provided for by a penalty. So had the case of the player resorting to the device of playing a strange ball from the rough, where his own was visible, for the purpose of testing the conditions for the stroke and the range of the green—or, in other words, making a practice stroke.

There were, then, very good reasons why the wrong-ball rule should be altered. In a match a golfer playing the wrong ball could benefit in two ways. If he played his opponent's ball by mistake, the opponent's ball would naturally be "lost," and under the rules of the day that meant loss of the hole. On the other hand, if the ball played wrongly was a stray, the golfer playing it had saved himself (if undetected) from the consequences of losing his own ball.

It was necessary to provide for these matters and also to guard against deliberate evasion, and it was in the light of this necessity that the rule was evolved and developed.

It may be argued that, since most "wrong balls" are played in error, the penalties (loss of the hole in match-play and two strokes in stroke-play) are unnecessarily harsh, and there is something to be said for the idea of making the punishment fit the crime by imposing progressive penalties. In this way there could be a penalty of one stroke in both match-play and stroke-play for one stroke played with the wrong ball, the full penalty being received for occasions when the player plays more than one stroke or holes out with the wrong ball.

Between 1888 and 1902, when the newly formed Rules of Golf Committee laid the foundations of the modern rules, there was a big spread in the popularity of golf and a consequent increase in the cases of playing stray balls in error. So the 1902 code, stipulating that a golfer playing the opponent's ball should lose the hole with no penalty if the opponent then played the other ball, was elaborated by this additional paragraph:

If a player play a stroke with the ball of a party not engaged in the match and the mistake be discovered and intimated to his opponent before the opponent has played his next stroke there should be no penalty. . . .

That rule, of course, applied only to matches, and in the same code we find a very liberal latitude given to the golfer playing a wrong ball in a stroke competition.

Special Stroke Rule No. 9 read:

A competitor shall hole out with his own ball at every hole, under penalty of disqualification. But if it be discovered before he has struck off from the next teeing ground (or, if the mistake occur at the last hole, before he has handed in his card) that he has not holed out with his own ball, he shall be at Liberty to return and hole out with his own ball, without penalty.

Honest John Low! He was the chief architect of that 1902 code and could not have imagined a golfer being so perverse as to use this latitude to his own ends by getting useful practice strokes without penalty. But the loophole was there and no doubt taken advantage of by many golfers, either inadvertently or deliberately. And the inevitable "tightening-up" process went on, so that by 1934 we find that, while the match-play rule has not altered, the Stroke Rule 9 is now much more severe. The first sentence remains, but the rest has given place to these two paragraphs:

If a competitor play a stroke or strokes with a ball other than his own he shall incur a penalty of two strokes. He shall then play his own ball.

In a hazard, if a competitor play a stroke or strokes with a ball other than his own, and the mistake be discovered before he has played a stroke with the wrong ball from outside the hazard, he shall incur no penalty provided he then play his own ball.

Having imposed the severe penalty of two strokes for slackness in not properly identifying a ball, the rule-makers realized that this would be harsh in the case of a ball in a hazard, which could not be lifted for identification.

In the experimental code of 1950 the wrong-ball rule was voluminous, tricky, and benevolent. In general, it imposed a penalty of one stroke if the action of playing the wrong ball did not damage the opponent (in match-play), but provided a penalty of loss of the hole if such action obliged the opponent to bring another ball into play under the impression his own was lost.

But there were several exceptions levying no penalty, on the understanding that in most cases where the action of playing the wrong ball was followed by similar action by an opponent, no advantage had been gained by either side.

In 1952 the experimental Rule 20 of more than 500 words became the present Rule 21 of less than half that length. But, if shorn of verbiosity, it was much more uncompromising in attitude. The penalty for playing the wrong ball (except in a hazard) was restored to two strokes in a stroke competition or loss of hole in a match, with the final penalty in stroke-play of disqualification if the error was not rectified by the player finding the right ball and playing it.

The 1952 rule did not state that strokes played with a wrong ball were not to be included in the score for the hole, but this was made clear in Decision 52/33 and the 1954 code amended accordingly.

In going from benevolence to austerity those who revised the 1950 code abandoned the provision

126

that the playing of a wrong ball in a match entailed no penalty if the other side immediately did likewise. But a case had soon to be considered where each player in a match had played the other ball in such circumstances that it was impossible to determine which side had erred first. This led to Decision 52/33 that "in equity" the hole should stand as played, and to the following Note to Rule added in 1954:

> When the player and the opponent exchange balls, the first to play the wrong one shall lose the hole; when this cannot be determined the hole shall be played out with the balls thus exchanged.

A curious aspect of Rule 21 was shown by Decision 53/42 concerning a player who thought his ball had finished in a water hazard, played another ball which he had dropped behind the hazard, and then found his original ball outside the hazard. He had actually played the wrong ball, because the original ball, not being in the hazard or "lost," was still in play.

Many players are not aware of the fact that a ball is not "in play" between the finish of one hole and the start of the next.

Two players in a stroke competition exchanged balls but did not realize their mistake until they had driven off, each with the other's ball, from the next teeing-ground. A played his second shot and B, preparing to play the like, discovered he was about to play the ball which was the property of A. Under

127

the impression that they had played the "wrong balls" from the teeing-ground, they exchanged balls and played on.

In fact (Decision 55/64/14) neither had incurred a penalty until the exchange of balls, when of course each was penalized two strokes for playing the wrong ball.

Since the war there has been official insistence on the fact that the responsibility for playing the correct ball rests entirely with the player.

Of two players approaching a "blind" green, A thought her shot had gone over the green and B thought her ball would be on the green. B walked to the one ball on the green and said it was her ball. Without checking this, A searched around the green for the other ball, failed to find it, and gave up the hole. Then it was discovered the ball on the green belonged to A.

The ruling (Decision 54/19/28) was that A must suffer for her own carelessness in not first identifying the ball on the green. The fact that B made a wrong statement did not affect the case, since the only rule concerning wrong information refers to information about the number of strokes played.

In 1952 the Rules of Golf Committee, obviously concerned about the increasing incidence of wrong-ball cases, added a recommendation that "each player should put an identification mark on his ball."

Before starting a match it is usual for players to announce the make and markings of the balls they are using, but the trouble often occurs during the round when a player, through loss or damage, puts down another ball which happens to be identical in marking with another in the same match. There should be a greater tendency among golfers towards having their initials stamped on the balls. Such a practice, if generally followed, would not only prevent mistakes but also facilitate the return of lost balls to their rightful owners.

CHAPTER XI

Things in the Way

FROM time immemorial it has been an inherent principle of golf that one's progress from teeing-ground to putting-green, if accurate, should be as free as possible from hazard.

But "accurate" in this context does not necessarily mean "straight."

In the very early days when courses lay over rough country, the "fair green" was restricted and beset, but gradually a pattern of the fairway would develop at each hole in accordance with the configuration of the ground and other circumstances. Such a pattern would be sometimes straightforward and sometimes devious, but if followed faithfully would enable the player to reach the green with minimum inconvenience and in the right number of strokes.

The ancient links of St. Andrews provide several

examples, the most obvious being the fourteenth,
the Long Hole In, where the drive is straight between the Beardies and the Wall, the second shot is
to the left, skirting Hell, and the third shot to the pin
is on the opposite tack.

At the other extreme is the ultra-simple hole on
a modern man-made course which encourages the
straight line and punishes deviation.

But, whatever line to the hole might be indicated or enforced, it has always been conceded that,
while a player might suffer from the consequences of
an ill-struck or ill-aimed stroke, or be unlucky
enough to suffer a rub of the green, he ought not to
be penalized for being obstructed by objects which
are not part of the course and which he might reasonably expect not to encounter.

An obstruction is defined as anything artificial,
whether erected, placed, or left on the course. In the
old days various attempts were made to list obstructions, and in 1851 the only ones mentioned were
clothes and washing-tubs.

"When a ball is on clothes or within a club-
length of a washing-tub," ran the rule, "the clothes
may be drawn from under the ball and the tub may
be removed."

This was clearly applying to local conditions at
St. Andrews, where the housewives were accustomed
to wash their linen in the Swilcan Burn (hence the
name) and to use the "fair green" of the first and
eighteenth holes as a drying-ground.

Some time during the next thirty years, with golfers "drawing clothes from under the ball" and no doubt soiling them in the process, there must have been many outcries from housewives, for in 1888 the rule was changed:

"When a ball lies on clothes the ball may be lifted and dropped behind without penalty."

Three years later the rule was changed again to have a meaning more or less equivalent to that of the present day: allowing the removal of movable obstructions or the removal of a ball lying on or touching an obstruction.

So far there had been no attempt to define obstructions, but the code of 1892 listed the following: flagstick, guide-flag, movable guide-post, wheelbarrow, tool, roller, grass-cutter, box, vehicle, "or similar obstruction." In 1934 the list included bridges, seats, huts and shelters, drain-covers, hydrants, and water-pipes.

In their own code issued just after the Second World War, the U.S.G.A. made a courageous attempt to list every possible obstruction and produced the following:

Any flagstick; sand-box; ball-washer; implement; stake; guide-post; vehicle; seat; shelter or similar obstruction (but not other buildings); clothes; artificial drains; drain covers; a hole made by a greenkeeper; material piled for removal, including a pile of leaves and cut grass; guy wires and other materials used to support trees; poles and other objects; artificial poles for electric wires;

132

artificial steps not made entirely of earth, but not steps of buildings which are not classified as obstructions under this Rule; bridges and abutments; protective screens; ropes and railings; stakes defining hazards and boundaries, but not fences or fence posts; parts of water systems and their covers, containers, bases and supports including fountains, pumps, pump houses, tanks, valves, hose and sprinklers; traps for insects or animals; boards for scores and notices; tents; refreshment stands; paper, bottles and similar artificial objects.

Whew!

What a wonderful example of how sensible business and professional men can get tangled up in verbiage of their own making. One can imagine this particular effort being given short shrift at the 1951 Anglo-American conference, where all this growth was cut away and the simple present definition introduced, with a guide to the procedure to be adopted according to whether the obstruction is movable or not.

The Rules do not give any guide, however, to the means of distinguishing between movable and immovable obstructions. Indeed, it would appear to be a question easily decided by observation or practical test. But it has been found necessary from time to time, particularly during championships or tournaments when stakes and fences are erected to control spectators, to label as "immovable" obstructions which are palpably movable.

During one Open Championship at St. Andrews,

133

a competitor whose ball lay near one of these stakes removed the stake, played his stroke, and then replaced the stake. But the stakes had been declared "immovable" by the Championship Committee, and since this fact obliged the player to obtain relief by moving his ball, not the obstruction, he was penalized two strokes for a breach of rule.

Many golfers are under the impression that because Rule 31 provides some measure of relief from an obstruction on which the ball is lying or which interferes with the player's stance or swing, they are entitled to a clear line to the hole. This is not so. A player, in removing his ball to within two club-lengths of "that point on the outside of the obstruction near which the ball originally lay," is not permitted to measure through the obstruction.

While every facility is afforded the golfer for evading the hardship of occasional obstruction or the temporary effects of weather (casual water, for example), there is no disposition to relieve the plight of one who is trapped in recognized hazards, whether artificial or natural.

Long years ago hazards abounded on the links. Indeed, everything except the fair green and the hole green was composed of hazards, even the heather. Even as late as 1891, when a hazard was defined for the first time, it was described as "any bunker of whatever nature, water, sand, loose earth, molehills, paths, roads, railways, whins, bushes, rushes, rabbit scrapes, fences, ditches, or anything which is not the ordinary green of the course (except blown or sprinkled sand, bare patches, and snow or ice)."

Now Definition 14 limits the hazard to "any bunker or water hazard," and specifically excepts scrapes, roads, tracks, and pathways.

Heather and whins (or what is usually known as gorse) are not mentioned because they are now classed as areas of rough country to which Rule 17 applies. And railways are not mentioned because they are not usually found within the boundaries of the course. And if they were, they would be in the same category as roads and paths, which are not now hazards and on which the club may be grounded.

Bunkers in the early days were depressions in the sand-dunes or earthly hollows made by nature, and usually fairly uncomfortable places from which to recover. The loose sand was usually heaped, furrowed, and pock-marked by wind, animals, and man, and the golfer had to play his ball as he found it.

Since being bunkered was an obstacle not easily overcome, the early rules were not greatly concerned with making things more difficult than they were, and the 1882 code stated merely that "when a ball is in a bunker, sand, or other hazard, there shall be no impression made by the club while addressing the ball, nor sand nor other obstacle removed before striking at the ball."

By 1902 the rule had become more or less what it is today, the basic principle still being that a player must not be permitted to improve the lie of the ball or test the consistency of the sand before making a stroke. He may not touch the sand at the address because this would allow him to remove or press down sand and so virtually "tee-up" the ball, or, by feeling the sand, gain some idea of how to play the shot. And since these are the only reasons for the opening paragraph of the present rule, it is stated that a player may place his clubs in a bunker provided he does nothing to improve the lie. A player accidentally dropping his club in a bunker (Decision 57/10/4) has also been absolved.

There is no penalty if a player smooths his footprints or club-marks after playing a stroke in a bunker, but if he does so and thereby improves the lie of the ball he has infringed the rule. For example, a player might fail to recover at the first attempt and then smooth his footmarks. If he fails a second time and the ball rolls back on to the smoothed sand, he would be held to have improved the lie or "assisted the subsequent play of the hole."

On the question of testing sand, two decisions issued about forty years ago are worth quoting. A player at Lee-on-Solent who grounded his club in a bunker about four yards from his ball was ruled to have lost the hole by "testing the sand." In another case while a foursome player was preparing to play out of the bunker his partner made a practice swing, taking sand, about three yards away in the same bunker, to show how the shot should be made. It

Too many golfers are too ready to declare the ball unplayable. Not so Paul H. Hohanson of Seattle, Washington, shown here during the 1952 Amateur Championship on his home course. He might never have heard of the ancient rule that "the ball must be played where it lies or the hole be given up." But in playing from twenty feet up this Douglas fir to the ninth green, he was acting in the spirit of all golf rules past and present—and he halved the hole.

An unidentified player playing a shot from the lip of a boiling cauldron, a unique hazard, on one of the most unusual golf courses in the world, the Arikikapakapa links in the Rotorua thermal district of Auckland Province, New Zealand.

If it had not plugged from the pitch, the ball would have bounded on or jumped back over the hole, or perhaps just dropped into the can. Impossible to say, so Definition 4 must be applied. A ball is not "holed" until it "lies within the circumference of the hole and all of it is below the level of the lip of the hole."

You might expect this kind of lie at Pinehurst, North Carolina, if not for a high-calibre player like Henry Picard. But even the great have their problems. This one was "to play or not to play," and Picard quite properly plays.

was ruled that the pair lost the hole because, although the golfer who had to play the stroke had not himself "tested the sand," his partner had gained information which could have been passed on.

Sand is less affected than water by the vagaries of weather and circumstance, so the rules regarding water hazards are more complex and less easily understood by golfers than those concerning sand bunkers.

Water has always played a part in the game of golf, except perhaps at the nineteenth hole. At Leith, where the earliest known written rules originated, there was water and "watery filth" which required legislation. And at St. Andrews, where the dunes and short-cropped turf offered little foothold for moisture, the Swilcan Burn and the Eden River were hazards, as they are today, although fewer golfers go into the Eden; and the Burn, then a natural creek running to the sea, is now a conduit confined in concrete.

As we have seen, there has always been a rule concerning a ball in water, but for a long time there was no distinction between permanent water hazards and casual water. Not until 1899, indeed, were there separate rules, and prior to that date there had been no mention of recognized water hazards.

In the 1888 code, the subject was covered in twenty-eight words: "If the ball lie in water the player may take it out, change it if he pleases, drop it and play from behind the hazard, losing a stroke."

In the 1899 code the rule for water was more detailed and included a statement that a recognized water hazard remained such even if it contained no water. This was obviously necessary since the construction of courses on arable land and in parks had brought irrigation ditches and ponds into the scheme of things, and without some rule regarding the limits of such hazards there would have been endless disagreement among players according to climatic conditions.

A water hazard does not cease to be one because the water therein has been reduced by drought; nor are its limits arbitrarily extended if flood-water overflows beyond the banks. If the ball lies within the stated limits, even on dry grass, it is in a water hazard. Similarly, if it lies outside the limits of the hazard but in flood-water, it must be treated as a ball in casual water.

In the revised code of 1920, and until after the Second World War, the rule of procedure for recovery applied to all water hazards, wherever situated. The player, if he did not wish to play the ball as it lay, had to drop a ball under a penalty of one stroke behind the hazard, keeping the spot at which the original ball crossed the margin of the hazard between himself and the hole.

Now, of course, we have a distinction between "water hazard" and "lateral water hazard," the latter being defined as one running approximately parallel to the line of play and so situated that it is deemed (by the Committee of the club) impracticable to drop a ball behind the water hazard and keep the spot where the ball last crossed the hazard margin between the player and the hole.

A ball in a lateral water hazard may be dropped within two club-lengths on either side of the hazard, opposite the point where the ball last crossed the margin.

Prior to 1934 a player in a water hazard could obtain relief only by dropping a ball behind or in the hazard under penalty. From 1934 to 1949 he was given the alternative of going back to play another ball under the stroke-and-distance rule, but only if the original ball had been played from a teeing-ground.

In 1950 under the St. Andrews code he was allowed to invoke the stroke-and-distance rule no matter from what part of the course the original ball had been played, but the United States adhered to the old rule. On both sides of the Atlantic, however, there had been difficulties over the water-hazard rules, and in the 1950 British code the trouble was tackled by distinguishing between transverse water hazards and lateral water hazards. In the United States they were content at that time to add the following paragraph to their existing rule:

If it be impossible for the player to drop a ball in conformity with this rule he shall drop as nearly as possible within the limits laid down but not nearer the hole.

If to drop a ball in conformity with rule may result in a ball becoming unplayable or unfairly difficult to play, then a local rule should state where the ball may be dropped. . . .

Later the U.S.G.A. agreed to adopt our rule which separated the two types of hazard. But it may be thought that even the present rule is unnecessarily detailed and confusing. Surely all that is needed is to ensure that the player, if he takes a ball from a water hazard, should be obliged to play over the hazard if it is across the line of play, or from a place not nearer the hole if the hazard is parallel to the line of play.

It sometimes happens that a ball enters a water hazard on the side nearer the hole, as, for example, when a player plays too strongly from a position behind the green into a hazard fronting the green. According to Decision 56/52/12, a ball in such circumstances should be played as it lies, or, if taken out under Rule 33(2), must be dropped on the far side of the hazard, so that the next stroke be made over the hazard towards the hole.

In the case of a golfer who hit a ball out of bounds from a water hazard (Decision 52/17) it was ruled that he must drop a ball in the hazard and then either play it out under stroke-and-distance penalty, or drop behind under an additional penalty of one stroke.

Since the demise of the floater we do not often

encounter the problem of a ball being moved by
water, but there was a case of a ball driven into a
fast-running brook being carried downstream beyond
the boundary of the course.

The ruling (Decision 56/80/35) was that the
ordinary rule applied. It was a fact that the ball
entered the water in bounds and therefore it should
have been dropped opposite the spot where it
entered the water.

It has also been made clear (Decision 53/30/51)
that a ball cannot be treated as lost in a water hazard
unless there is reasonable evidence that the ball
lodges therein; and that if the player and his opponent disagree, there is too much doubt for Rule 33 to
apply.

A similar case (Decision 53/–/42) concerned a
player who, believing his ball to be in a water hazard,
dropped a ball behind and played it towards the
green. He then found his original ball outside the
hazard. It was ruled that he must abandon the
second ball, continue play with the original ball, and
also suffer two strokes penalty for playing the wrong
ball.

We have seen how the rules prevent the golfer
from obtaining relief without penalty from the
natural difficulties of the course, and how they give
him relief, without penalty, if he be impeded by
artificial difficulties.

Now we have to consider how the rule applies
to difficulties which, whether natural or artificial, are

merely temporary and not numbered among the permanent features of the links.

These are grouped under three heads—Casual Water, Ground Under Repair, and Holes Made by a Burrowing Animal—and from their very nature it is clear that none of them is more difficult than the task of defining them. The history of the last fifty years shows that even the law-makers have not found it easy to legislate fairly, and the average golfer continues to be puzzled by some aspects of Rule 32.

Casual water, according to the latest definition, is "any temporary accumulation of water which is visible before or after a player has taken his stance," and it is held to include snow and ice.

Water, as we have seen, is one of the oldest hazards in golf, but only in recent years has it been thought fit to distinguish between the permanent and casual states.

In 1888 the rule was uncompromising, but by 1902 the distinction between water hazards and casual water was recognized by relief being given without penalty if a ball lay in casual water anywhere, or if casual water intervened between ball and hole on the putting-green. And casual water was defined for the first time as "any temporary accumulation of water which is not one of the ordinary and recognized hazards of the course."

In 1950 this became "any temporary accumulation of water which is not within the margin of a water hazard."

The present definition was introduced in 1956 following the experience of four years including a much-discussed incident at Muirfield during the 1954 Amateur Championship.

J. B. Carr of Ireland, playing Peter Toogood of Australia, found his ball in marshy ground on the left of the second fairway. By treading in the grass Carr caused water to appear and claimed it to be casual water. But there was a doubt whether or not the marshy area was caused by a spring and therefore permanent. After inspection, officials decided it was casual water.

One of the points raised on this occasion was whether water, before being declared "casual," had to be visible on the surface of the ground. The question was at least fifty years old, for under the 1902 rules a club wanted to know whether casual water had to be deep enough "for a ball to float in it." The answer then was that casual water came under the definition if it interfered with the lie of the ball or the stance of the player.

Casual water may be present but not visible until the player treads on the area, and referees and committees, asked for rulings on the spot, have usually taken the view that if water wells up above the soles of the shoes as the player takes his stance it comes under the definition. That is substantially the meaning behind the present definition.

The introduction of "ground under repair" is also of comparatively recent occurrence. The rules of

1857 contained no reference to such an area, but in
1888 the following rule was included: "If a ball lies
in any of the holes made for golfing, or on ground
under repair by the conservators of the links, it may
be lifted, dropped behind the hazard, and played
without losing a stroke."

More than sixty years went by, however, before
it was thought necessary to define "ground under
repair." Now it is ground "so marked by the committee or declared such by the authorities," and the
term is also held to cover material piled for removal
or a hole made by a greenkeeper "even if not so
marked."

The latter part of the definition has been open to
very wide interpretation. The contents of a grass-
box dumped in the rough near a green are not necessarily "piled for removal." And from my own experience I can quote the case of a player whose ball
finished in a rhododendron bush, but who claimed
relief, and obtained it, because the ball lay on grass
mowings.

It was obvious that the mowings had been
thrown there with no intention of moving them elsewhere, and equally obvious that the player, to be
able to be "on ground which avoids these conditions,"
would have to drop outside the bush.

But I question the ethics of converting a palpably unplayable lie into a playable one by such
dubious means.

For similar reasons there have been many

queries and arguments over the third set of conditions quoted by Rule 32: "A Hole, Cast or Runway
Made by a Burrowing Animal, a Reptile or a Bird."

There is no attempt to define these in detail, for
the very good reason that only official inspection on
the spot by a qualified person could set all doubts at
rest.

What seems a rabbit-scrape to the player whose
ball lies in it might be regarded by his opponent as a
worn divot-mark. And the nature of a hole might
be equally open to argument.

The present phrase was adopted by the Americans in their own rules, prior to 1951, when it was
applied by agreement to the whole world of golf. But
in adopting it the Anglo-American committee ex-
cluded rabbit-scrapes, and this began a series of com-
plaints from golfers who could not distinguish between rabbit-scrapes and "casts or runways."

And since a rabbit making a scrape is going
through the motions of starting a hole, I propounded
the question: "When does a rabbit-scrape become a
rabbit-hole?"

The question was never answered, but four years
later the reservation about rabbit-scrapes was removed.

It was a victory for progressive thought over
tradition. Golfers who remembered that in 1812 a
player, while allowed to pick and drop without
penalty from rabbit-holes, had to play the ball from
a rabbit-scrape "as from any common hazard," were

losing ground to those who thought that golfers
were entitled to relief from accidental bad lies of that
kind.

The history of this rule should be remembered
as an example of the effects of trying to cater for
every contingency on a golf course, instead of letting
equity and honesty be the guides to conduct.

I do not think it right that a player should have
relief from every possible bit of trouble on the course,
and why he should get relief from a rabbit-scrape
and not from a divot-mark is beyond comprehension.

CHAPTER XII

The Flagstick

THE flagstick, states Definition 12, is "a movable indicator provided by the Committee, with or without bunting attached, placed in the hole to show its position."

Apart from leaving it open to doubt whether the bunting is to be attached to the flagstick or the Committee, there is a casual vagueness about this description which contrasts sharply with other definitions, including that for the hole in which the flagstick is placed. Yet recent alterations in the rules have promoted the flagstick to be a very important item in the game.

It must be conceded, nevertheless, that the varied character of courses and sometimes the nature of the environment, as well as the idiosyncrasies of committees and the state of the club finances, all

have influences on the type, size, and quality of the
flagsticks used. In the very early days golfers were
content with primitive means of indicating the position of the hole, and a branch broken from a near-by
bush or hedgerow would serve as well as anything,
particularly with a wisp of cloth tied to the top.
From that device would evolve straight laths or
rounded poles carrying pennants or flags. Fifty years
ago it was common for golf courses to be also grazing
grounds for sheep and cattle, and the flagsticks were
mounted on spiral springs so that they would not be
broken or the hole damaged by animals pushing
against them. Spring-loaded flagsticks were often
useful, too, on courses where high winds on exposed
greens would snap rigid poles.

The use of the phrase "bunting or other material" is a reminder that half a century ago the use of
a flag was by no means universal, and even between
the wars the "flagsticks" at the Ranelagh Club,
Barnes, were surmounted by egg-shaped wicker
baskets which somehow seemed to fit into the scheme
of statuary and lily-ponds on that short yet intriguing
course.

In length of stick, too, there has been endless
variation, even among the flagsticks used on one
course. This is due sometimes to the configuration of
the ground, since the flagstick on a green with a
blind approach should be tall enough for the flag to be
visible from a distance. And in the matter of environ-

ment most suburban clubs know the troubles caused by the raids of mischievous children and vandals.

When Ben Hogan was at Carnoustie winning the Open Championship he told me the varying heights of the flagsticks had some effect on his approach play. He is accustomed to judge distances to the green by using the flagsticks as a surveyor would use distance posts, and on American courses, he assured me, all the "pins" were of uniform height. That may be true, but in Britain there has been no attempt to prescribe limits for the dimensions of a flagstick. The official view seems to be that if it fulfils its function of indicating the position of the hole, clubs may please themselves as to the design, but in the first two years after the new flagstick rule was introduced in 1956 there were so many examples of the need for uniformity that some action by the Rules of Golf Committee would have seemed to be desirable.

Rule 34 now allows the player to have the flagstick left unattended in the hole, and if his ball strike the flagstick in such circumstances, no matter from how short a distance, there is no penalty. Now, on some courses the flagsticks are so thick that no ball on striking one could possibly fall into the hole or be wedged between stick and holeside, to drop when the stick is removed. On other courses the sticks are so thin that a ball striking one with moderate force would either drop completely or fall on removal of the stick. It may be a matter of opinion whether a golfer, now getting some protection from the consequences of a straight putt struck with too much strength, should also be able to hole out with a ball which, but for the flagstick in the way, would have run over the hole. But, whatever the general view of what is right and proper, it will be conceded that uniformity is desirable.

My own idea is that the thickness of the pin, at least from the base to a point some inches above the turf, should be one inch. This would give, between the outside of the pin and the inside of the hole, a space of just over the diameter of the ball. With such a pin in an upright position, the ball struck with just sufficient force to reach the hole would drop in on removal of the pin, but if struck with greater strength, would probably rebound and stay out. On exposed courses a flagstick one inch thick for all its length might be too thin, but the standard thickness need apply only to the lower portion. And there are several good types of tubular metal sticks on the market strong enough to remain straight in all weathers.

Another point concerns the angle at which the flagstick stands in the hole. It has been decreed (Decision 56/8/2) that a golfer may play at a mal-adjusted flagstick as it stands or may adjust it to a vertical position before playing. But he is not per-mitted to adjust it to an abnormal position, varying from the vertical, to give himself an undue advantage in holing out. That is held to be an infringement of Rule 35(1*h*) prohibiting action which might influence the action of the ball.

Some flagsticks, replaced carelessly by the previous couple or blown sideways by the wind, could be found in a slanting position. If the slant is away from the player, he will have a slight advantage with an accurate putt because the space between pin and hole-edge is wider than normal. On the other hand, if the slant is towards the player, his chances of holing out are correspondingly slight. These are very good reasons for the decision just quoted, but I am not too happy about the freedom given the player to handle the flagstick and still putt at an "unattended" stick. One of the ideas behind the new Rule 34 was to save time and handling, and that end will be defeated if players are allowed to spend time on adjusting slanting flagsticks.

On the other hand, it is necessary to legislate for the possibility, however remote, of the flagstick being left maladjusted by a preceding player seeking to place the player at a disadvantage, or even an opponent in the same match doing so.

Bearing in mind all the considerations, it is becoming clear that with the flagstick playing so important a part in the game it should be standardized not only in size but also in construction, so that when replaced it automatically takes up a vertical position.

Many courses have now been fitted with combination sets of hole-linings and pins so constructed that the lower end of the pin is held upright in a socket extending below the base of the hole-lining.

These criticisms apart, the new Rule 34 is a great improvement on previous legislation. It was always an injustice that so much could happen to a player because, as a gesture of courtesy, he attended the pin while his opponent played. A little tardiness, a slight lack of agility, and he could lose the hole by allowing the opponent's ball to strike the flagstick.

Now the responsibility for what happens to the flagstick is placed entirely on the shoulders of the golfer about to play. He can have it attended or not as he pleases. If his ball strikes an unattended flagstick, there is no penalty. If his ball strikes a flagstick attended, no matter by whom, the player is penalized, not the individual at the stick.

It is important to realize that this alteration cancels the right previously enjoyed by a golfer to attend the flagstick while his opponent or fellow competitor is playing. He may do so now only at the request of the player. This, of course, marks a very big development in the course of about seventy years. The flagstick came into the rules in 1888 in this way:

> If, in holing out, the ball shall rest upon the flagstick in the hole, the player shall be entitled to have the stick removed; and if the ball fall in it shall be considered as holed out; but either party is entitled to have the flagstick removed when approaching the hole.

In 1899 a new stroke rule was introduced reading:

When a competitor's ball is within 20 yards of the hole the competitor may not play until the flag has been removed, under penalty of one stroke.

This rather elliptical treatment was altered in 1908 to read:

When a competitor's ball, lying within 20 yards of the hole, is played and strikes or is stopped by the flagstick or the person standing at the hole, the penalty shall be two strokes.

But in the rules governing match-play in that era (1908–20) it was laid down that "either side is entitled to have the flagstick removed when approaching the hole; if a player's ball strike the flagstick which has been so removed by himself or his partner, or either of their caddies, his side shall lose the hole." This particular rule did not prescribe any penalty if the opponent was holding the flagstick, but that was provided for by another rule involving loss of the hole by the opponent if he or his caddie were struck by the player's ball while in motion.

It was not until the revision of 1934 that the penalty of loss of the hole was specifically prescribed for the case of a ball striking a flagstick held or removed by the opponent or his caddie.

As with all new rules, No. 34 in the 1956 code

has been imperfectly understood by many golfers and produced a proportionately large number of decisions. It has, in any case, always been difficult for the ordinary golfer to understand his responsibilities, commitments, and liabilities when on or near the putting-green, mainly because it is necessary to have different procedure for match- and medal-play. But the new rule is shorter and more to the point than most of its predecessors and has the virtue that each of its four paragraphs applies to both match- and medal-play, the only difference being in the nature of the penalties.

The chief misunderstanding has been about the right of the player to full control of the flagstick. Although this is implied, it is not specifically stated in the rule, and it has been necessary to point out by decisions that if a player fails to exercise this right, by allowing the stick to be held or attended against his wishes or inclination, he must be deemed to have consented to such action. This and other rulings suggest that some clarification will be necessary when the next rules revision takes place.

It has been ruled, for instance (Decision 56/79/52), that a player who has putted with the flagstick unattended may instruct his caddie to remove the flagstick while his ball is in motion. On the face of it this seems to be out of tune with the provisions of Rule 35 (Putting-Green), which prohibits the lifting or touching of an opponent's ball while the

154

player's ball is in motion, and also forbids player and caddie taking any action to influence the position or the movement of the ball. On the other hand, it has been ruled rightly (Decision 56/122/49) that an opponent rushing to grab an unattended flagstick while a player's ball is in motion loses the hole for having held the flagstick without the consent of the player.

The contrary case of an attended flagstick being abandoned with the ball in motion has also been the subject of a decision (56/23/8). The partner of a player putting in a fourball match first went to the flagstick (although not on any request by his partner) and during the stroke walked away from the flagstick, which was struck by the ball. It was ruled that the player, although not having called for the flagstick to be attended, tacitly consented to this being done, and must suffer the penalty for striking an "attended" flagstick.

In the case of a player who was not sure whether a caddie standing near the hole intended to attend the flagstick, it is stated (Decision 56/12/24) that: "If before playing a player sees someone in the match standing near the flagstick and does not tell him to stand clear he must be deemed to have given his consent to the flagstick being attended."

Many thinking golfers are concerned about the way in which the rules have grown in volume during the past fifty years, and would welcome some means of reducing them to proportions which would tempt the average player to become acquainted with them. Yet two years' experience of a simplified flagstick rule, foreshadowing the necessity for clarifying and embellishing the four simple paragraphs of which it consists, does not encourage the hope of a "code for the common man" in the foreseeable future.

CHAPTER XIII

The Putting-Green

TWENTIETH-CENTURY golfers accustomed to criticizing the greenkeeper if the putting-surfaces of their courses are not smooth as bowling-greens find it difficult, indeed impossible, to realize that putting the ball into the hole from even a few feet in the eighteenth century was not merely a question of stroking it in with a putter.

The term "putting-green" is, in fact, of comparatively modern origin. Two hundred years ago it was called the "hole-green" and was merely a patch of grass cropped by rabbits and selected by the original course "designers" as a suitable place for making the hole. And its condition after a few hours of use may be imagined from the fact that the player, having holed out, had to tee up for the next drive not more than one club's length away. The tee itself would be made from sand (usually taken from the bottom of the hole just used), but this would not protect the turf from being damaged by schlaffing clubheads and the feet of the players, so that holing out from one yard was actually as difficult in those days as many golfers make it seem to be today. If we are to believe the pictorial records of even a hundred years ago, there were also the additional complications of pressing humanity (at any rate, on big occasions), with the poor player hemmed in on all sides by partner, opponents, caddies, and gambling spectators, to say nothing of little girls hawking ginger-beer.

Recalling those glimpses of long ago, one wonders again at the sensitivity of modern players, who animadvert against camera-men fifty yards away, require complete hush from a gallery ringed twenty yards from the hole, and want new holes cut every day because the turf around has been under the pressure of feet. The only complaint their great-great-grandfathers made was that so much sand for tees was taken from the bottom of the hole in use that it was often difficult to recover the ball after holing out! Indeed, it is within the memory of golfers living today when the golf-hole was not standardized in dimensions. And the use of a proper lining is probably no older than the Open Championship.

The first mention of standard dimensions for the hole was in the code of 1891, which laid down the diameter as 4¼ inches and the depth as 4 inches—measurements which have persisted to this day.

The arbitrary diameter of 4¼ inches is said to have originated from the bright idea of two St. Andrews golfers who, noticing one hole particularly badly worn by the removal of sand for making tees, found a piece of drain-pipe lying near and inserted it in the hole to form a permanent "cup." The diameter of the pipe happened to be 4¼ inches. How much mortification would have been saved the world of golf if it had been an inch wider!

By 1891 the extent of the putting-green had been defined, but before that the area had been very loosely described. In 1851 the putting-green was mentioned for the first time by this paragraph: "All loose impediments of whatever kind may be lifted from the putting-green or tableland on which the hole is placed, and which is considered not to exceed twenty yards from the hole." In 1888 the definition was more precise—"those portions of the links devoid of hazards within twenty yards of the hole"— and this, with slight variations in wording, remained the official definition until the Anglo-American revision of 1952, when the following form was adopted:

The "putting-green" is all ground of the hole being played which is specially prepared for putting or otherwise defined as such by the Committee.

Under the earlier definition there were some obvious absurdities. In certain circumstances, according to where the hole was cut, a ball might have been legally on the putting-green while nestling in deep rough or even in the middle of a bush.

A century ago, when greenkeeping was neither the fine art it is today nor so well equipped mechanically, it was no doubt difficult on some courses to distinguish the "surface specially prepared for putting" from the surrounding turf. But the archaic "twenty yards" definition was allowed to remain long after the special need for it had passed. The current definition was invoked in a recent decision (53/–/33) concerning a course where the ninth green was adjacent to the eighteenth green but separated from it by a narrow strip of ground not "specially prepared for putting." A player in a stroke competition whose ball landed on the ninth green when he was playing to the eighteenth putted his ball across from one green to the other and claimed in justification that the situation was no different from that at St. Andrews and some other courses where double greens were in use. He was penalized two strokes by his club committee for not lifting his ball and dropping it clear of what was "a putting-green other than that of the hole being played." This decision was upheld by the Rules of Golf Committee, who pointed out that the greens in question had been defined by the local committee as separate greens and so could not be likened to the double greens of St. Andrews.

By 1851, as the rules introduced in that year constantly remind us, the game was taking its present shape, and from then onwards to the end of the nineteenth century the rules regarding putting were elaborated as succeeding generations of golfers found the need for providing for various contingencies. The improvement in putting-surfaces, for example, is reflected by the introduction in 1851 of the first rule to cover "loose impediments," which by that time were much more noticeable on the sizable greens of cropped or scythed or mown turf than they had been to the golfers of 1744 on "greens" no bigger than a card table.

But the rules of 1851 did not define "loose impediments," and no doubt in succeeding years golfers had great argument on such subjects. For in 1888 we find that if ice or snow lie on the green, "parties are recommended to make their own arrangements for its removal or not before commencing the match." This did not mean a discussion whether or not to hire men with shovels to clear the course, but whether or not to agree to ice and snow being moved from the line of the putt.

Three years later the rule stipulating the removal of loose impediments by the hand alone was relaxed to permit the use of the club in removing dung. Now, of course, anything on the line of the putt may be picked up or brushed aside either by hand or club, so long as there is no pressure on the turf.

From the turn of the century the complexities of putting increased rapidly, and now Rule 35, relating to play and procedure on the putting-green, is easily the longest in the book, despite the fact that the regu-

lations regarding the flagstick, at one time incorporated under the heading of Putting-Green, now form
a separate rule. Such paragraphs as those regarding
loose impediments, touching the line of the putt,
placing a mark for putting, and testing the surface
of the green are all sprung from the improvement in
putting-surfaces. It has also been necessary to alter
from time to time the rules covering the lifting and
marking of balls interfering with or assisting the play
of another player. For this we have to thank the development of stroke-play and the abolition of the
stymie.

Before written rules existed, there was probably
no question of lifting the ball in a match and it was
a case of every man for himself. A ball lying in the
way of the other, or lying near it in such a position
that a stroke was impeded, was something which had
to be suffered or turned to advantage, as no doubt
it was in cases where the ball nearer the hole could
be sent further away from the hole by the execution
of a stroke more suitable to croquet or billiards than
to golf.

In the Edinburgh code of 1744 some attempt
was made to provide for such contingencies by Rule
6: "If your balls be found anywhere touching one another you are to lift the first ball till you play the
last" and by Rule 7: "At holing you are to play your
ball honestly for the hole, and not to play on your
adversary's ball, not lying in your way to the hole."

Nearly fifty years afterwards, in 1789, what has

become known as the "stymie rule" was first introduced. It was laid down that "In all time coming, in case in playing over the links any ball shall lye in the way of his opponent's at the distance of six inches upon the hole green, it shall be in the power of the party playing to cause his opponent to move said ball." This strange mixture of verbose ambiguity and staccato directness existed until 1833, when it was agreed to abandon the stymie and allow all balls on the putting-green to be lifted at the option of the player about to putt. One year later this experiment was abandoned and the stymie reintroduced in a much more readable form by the following rule:

"When the balls lie within six inches of each other in any situation the ball nearest the hole to be lifted until the other is played." In one form or another this rule remained until in 1952, after much argument extending over many years, it vanished from the game.

Colonel M. E. Lindsay points out there were only two occasions when the word "stymie," known to golfers all over the world, has been mentioned in the rules.

In 1851 it was laid down that "all balls must be holed out on the Medal Days and no stymies allowed." In 1858 this was applied to all stroke-play, but on this occasion the word is spelt "stimie."

There have been several interesting attempts to pinpoint an etymological derivation of the word, but, like most other investigations of that kind, there can be only supposition without certainty. One writer, the late Robert Browning in his *A History of Golf*, was loyal to Burns and his use of the word "Styme" as signifying "blinded," and affected to disregard the Gaelic *Stigh mi,* meaning "inside me," or the Dutch *Stuit mij,* meaning "it stops me." But it is probable that Burns owed as much to the Gaelic and the Dutch as the stymie owes to Burns.

Whatever the derivation of the stymie, we can be certain of the circumstances of its demise, and confident too that no single factor in golf caused more exasperation by its existence nor more contention in its passing.

The early match-playing golfers, with their "break-clubs," courses full of hazards, and putting-greens used as teeing-grounds, regarded the ball "in the way" as just another hazard. But their descendants, encountering it on smooth putting-greens, regarded it with mixed feelings coloured by its impact on their chances of success. A golfer might be full of smug complacency on one green as he observed his ball sidle gently in between the hole and the opposing ball; and full of irritation on the next green to find that he himself had been "laid a stymie." The history of championship and international golf is littered with stories of great issues decided by stymies, and, as with most of these occurrences, the golfer tended to remember the times he had been stymied and forget the stymies he had laid other players.

When, between the wars, the Americans were drifting away from us in various matters, one of the chief bones of international contention was the stymie. The Americans, having less tradition, had a logical attitude towards the stymie as something which no one wanted and was foreign to modern ideas of golf. For some years they operated a partial no-stymie rule under which a ball in the way could be lifted, at the request of the player about to putt, if it lay within six inches of the hole. It was argued in support of this rule that a ball nearer to the hole than six inches was a complete bar, since it gave the player almost no hope of a successful loft.

In 1950 the United States Golf Association abandoned the stymie altogether, but St. Andrews retained it because, while there was obviously a fair amount of support for abolition among ordinary golfers, the Dominions and other governing bodies, being consulted, had shown "no great preponderance of opinion in favour of abolition."

This was perhaps the proper attitude for authority to adopt in circumstances which seemed to indicate a fairly even division between abolitionists and retentionists, but it did not take into account the obvious fact that, whatever governing bodies might think, the great mass of golfers disliked the stymie and would welcome abolition.

While the stymie "war" was being carried on between die-hards and modernists using all kinds of abstract arguments, there was the concrete fact that more and more friendly matches were being played on a "no-stymies" basis. Ordinary club golfers could not see why the way to the hole should be blocked on the putting-green by a ball which, had it lain anywhere else on the course and within a club-length, could have been lifted; why, having gone through difficulties and hazards on their way to the green, they could not be entitled to a clear putt; or again why, since they could lift all manner of loose impediments between their ball and the hole, the opponent's ball, a most obstructive impediment, could not be touched.

Nor, in this new spirit of the game, with a vast new golfing population having no roots in the past, could tradition plead successfully in defence of the stymie. It was outmoded, out-argued, and soon to be outvoted. When the Anglo-American discussions took place in 1949, the supporters of the stymie made a dignified retreat and the long contention was ended.

But the act of abolition brought new problems in its train. The first no-stymie rule stated that the ball nearer the hole "could be lifted without penalty at the option of the owner or the opponent, if either consider it might interfere with or be of assistance to the player." Golfers were now given the freedom to move the ball and did so at every conceivable opportunity, often when it was unnecessary. This practice not only caused delay, but also opened the door to abuse, since it was possible for a player to clean a ball which had been lifted, or shorten the length of his putt by adroit manipulation of ball and marking-disc.

Both in the United States and Great Britain there were discussions on how to check this spate of "lifting and marking," and in 1956 the present rule was introduced, preventing the owner of the nearer ball from lifting it except at the request of the player about to putt.

Thus, without reverting to the stymie, we returned a long way towards the days of the stymie, since the ball nearer the hole once more became a factor in play. It might be argued that the new rule was to the advantage of the player, because in certain circumstances he could "use" the ball nearer the hole while still retaining the right to have it out of the way. But if the owner of the nearer ball, having putted, had left his ball in a position where it would be "used" by his opponent, he ought to be prepared to accept the circumstances. In any case, since it ensured the greatest good for the greatest number, the new rule must be regarded as a valuable contribution to the smoother running of the game.

In stroke competitions the position is slightly different and the change in rule not quite so beneficial. The competitor about to putt may have the nearer ball lifted or played, at the option of the owner of that ball, if he consider it interferes with his play.

The owner of the ball may not lift it unless so requested, but if he consider it might be of assistance to the player, he may putt out first.

At first sight this suggests a means of restricting lifting and marking at least to as great an extent as in match-play. But in practice it has been found less effective than was hoped, for two reasons. First, as already suggested, because a ball which would be of assistance in a match would be a possible danger in a stroke competition, and therefore the stroke competitor tends to have any ball lifted which could by any stretch of the imagination be in danger of being struck by his own ball. Secondly, there has grown up a general practice of players assuming that the competitor wishes the ball to be lifted, and the competitor tacitly agreeing to that suggestion because it is, if anything, an advantage to him to have the other ball out of the way.

A note to Rule 35(3*a*), concerning this point, recommends that the ball nearer the hole be played rather than lifted, unless the subsequent play of a fellow competitor is likely to be affected (by the other player having stood on his line to putt, for example). But in practice this is scarcely ever done, and so lifting and marking has gone on in stroke competitions more or less to the same extent as before.

One way to restrict this habit would be to apply more firmly the rule against lifting a ball in the absence of any request. In Decision 56/US/15, based on an incident in the United States, it was ruled that the owner of the nearer ball who lifted when not asked to do so had infringed the rules by touching or moving his ball purposely, and should be penalized two strokes. On the other hand, if he putted out when not asked to do so, he had merely played out of turn, which in stroke-play incurs no penalty.

One result of the increase in lifting and marking has been a more conscientious adherence by golfers to the proper marking procedure, with a coin or disc. The old days of match-sticks and pieces of dried grass are gone, although there are still cases of golfers scratching an arrow in the turf with finger or tee-peg before lifting the ball. Apart from its lack of precision as compared with a marker, this procedure not only damages the turf but also is a technical offence against Rule 35(1d) (testing the surface of the green). I should like to see St. Andrews adopt a more severe attitude towards marking by scratching and also to incorporate proper marking instructions in the rules. For instance, it should be a case for a penalty if a player marks his ball in any other way than by placing a coin or similar mark behind the ball before lifting, and by replacing the ball before lifting the marker.

One of the least understood putting-green rules reads:

When a player has holed out and his opponent has been left with a stroke for the half, nothing the player

who has holed out can do shall deprive him of the half
he has already gained.

This came into force in 1902 and has not often
been invoked, but a decision of 1913 may be quoted
as illustrating circumstances in which it operates.

Having holed out, A stood near to the hole while
B attempted to hole out for the half. B missed, and
at that moment A was the winner of the hole. But
the ball ran on and struck A's foot before he could
get out of the way. B claimed the hole, but A, having
already holed out, could not be deprived of the half
he had gained.

The Rules of Golf Committee of the time added
this footnote to the decision: "If 'A' had observed
Rule 1 of Etiquette (standing close to player) the
incident would not have happened."

Another decision has made it clear that the
giving of wrong information as to the number of
strokes played could not rob a player of the half
already gained. A third example was of a player who
holed out and, in recovering his ball, accidentally
moved his opponent's ball.

Our Victorian ancestors had to make frequent
changes in and additions to the putting-green rules to
keep pace with changing conditions. Now it is the
longest rule in the book, and still golfers, to judge
from the many requests for rulings, are nonplussed.
Sometimes it would seem almost desirable to return
to the "hole-green" of two centuries ago. Then the

short game had a proper relation to the long game. Today, when a putt of two feet can be more important than a 250-yard drive and, if missed, more destructive than a long iron shot into the rough, the putting-green is not only far too large an area on the course but also of far too great importance in the traditional scheme of golf.

CHAPTER XIV

Running the Game

THE first eleven rules in the present code may be regarded as the working principles of the game, those fundamentals which should guide the golfer's approach and keep him informed of his rights and responsibilities.

Into the same category fall the concluding rules, dealing with the organization of competitions and the conduct of players, and the various appendices, including those relating to amateurism and the form and make of clubs.

It follows from the character of these rules that their case-history is comparatively meagre. They are the respectable permanent provisions governing the "set-up," and respectability has no history. Nevertheless, they are so important that it is a matter for astonishment that they are of comparatively recent origin—in fact, no older than the code of 1908. In the early days golfers were concerned mainly with the enjoyment of their own matches under conditions mutually agreeable, and what happened on the course in the actual play was of far greater moment than abstract questions.

When rules became necessary because golf had spread beyond its former narrow confines and the integration of various golfing centres had started, they were framed with that consideration in view, and developed along similar lines for 150 years. But the spread of the game beyond the close coteries of sportsmen who had fostered it in the eighteenth century and particularly the growing popularity of stroke competitions rendered necessary the introduction of machinery for controlling all kinds of "off-the-course" activities.

This was gradually realized in the course of the revisions which took place from 1888 to 1902, but not until 1908 was there any large-scale attempt to provide rules for the over-all control of the game and particularly competitions. In that year the Rules of Golf blossomed into all their verbose glory, introduced by this comprehensive title-page:

RULES OF THE GAME OF GOLF

As approved by the Royal and Ancient
Golf Club of St. Andrews, September, 1908

together with
Recommendations

Form and Make of Golf Clubs
Etiquette
Special Rules for Match-play Competitions
Rules for three-ball and best ball matches and
Fourball Matches
Special Rules for Stroke Competitions

The "Recommendations" were intended to advise club committees on how far they could depart from the Rules of Golf in making local rules for local conditions. The heading "Form and Make of Golf Clubs" covered the following paragraph: "The Rules of Golf Committee intimates that it will not sanction any departure from the form and make of golf clubs which, in its opinion, consist of a plain shaft and a head which does not contain any mechanical contrivance such as springs!"

But there was this curiosity—the paragraph was quite separate from the rules, and the rules themselves included no provision for any penalty for playing with irregular clubs. It was not until much later that this was adjusted by the inclusion of an opening paragraph in the preamble to the rules:

The game of golf consists in a ball being played from the teeing-ground into the hole by successive strokes with clubs and balls made in conformity with the directions laid down in the clause on "Form and Make of Golf Clubs and Balls."

174

The clause itself was still printed apart from the rules, but the new Rule 1 dealing with matches and competitions stated:

In competitions players using clubs or balls which are not in conformity in the clause shall be disqualified.

This rather clumsy arrangement lasted for the whole of the period between the wars, but in the revision of 1950 and every subsequent code the whole business was streamlined by a complete Rule 2 giving detailed specifications of clubs and balls and laying down the penalty of disqualification for using illegal equipment. These developments and the "fourteen clubs" rule are discussed in other chapters.

Most of the other preliminary rules are self-explanatory, but some have been the subject of clubhouse debate and subsequent appeals to St. Andrews. For instance, it has always been difficult to make golfers understand that in a stroke competition the stipulated round must be played and that the stipulated round (Definition 29) consists in playing eighteen holes of the course in their correct order.

This is or should be obvious, but the position has been clarified by recent decisions, one of which makes it clear that the correct sequence must start at the first teeing-ground unless the committee in charge decide otherwise.

In the case of two players who started at the

175

fourteenth and played the last five holes of the round
and then the first thirteen in correct order, it was
ruled (Decision 55/106) that they must be disqualified. There is a distinct difference, in the
attitude of authority, between golfers altering the
stipulated round on their own initiative and those doing so with the prior consent of the committee, or on
official instructions. In the former case, unlimited
licence to please themselves would quickly create
confusion and lead to abuse. It is not always the case
that if a player holes out at every hole with the ball
played from the teeing-ground, he has completed the
stipulated round. In the case of a player who drove
out of bounds and continued playing that ball because he was not aware of the fact, it was ruled
(Decision 53/–/26) that the competitor had played
a ball not in play and, having failed to correct his
mistake before driving off the next tee, had not completed the stipulated round and was therefore disqualified.

Confusion also is common in the mind of the
average golfer about Practice Strokes. These are not
permitted during the play of a hole, nor between
holes if the stroke is played from any hazard or on to
any putting-green of any hole not yet played. So that
a player who had knocked back his fellow competitor's ball after the latter had failed to halve the
hole with bogey in a competition was adjudged innocent of any breach (Decision 53/57/48). And it
has also been established (Decision 52/2) that the

retrying of a putt in a stroke competition is permissible provided that the play at that hole has finished and the action does not delay play.

This liberty was held to be available (Decision 56/6/1) to a player on a nine-hole course who retried a putt on the second green, despite the fact that he would have to play that hole later on as the eleventh of the "full round." It was held that the injunction in Rule 8 Paragraph 2 should apply only to the "course round" of nine holes.

One of the most important recent additions to the rules, and one which is not understood by many golfers, is Paragraph 5 in Rule 11, dealing with Claims and Rights. It provides in stroke-play only an opportunity for a player in doubt as to his rights or how to proceed in any contingency, to play out the hole with the ball in play and at the same time complete the play of the hole with a second ball played under what he believes to be his rights.

The purpose of this rule is to save the player from running the risk of disqualification, but it also means a great saving in time. Often in important competitions players have been confronted by problems and, unwilling to risk disqualification by doing the wrong thing and not wishing to incur a penalty which might not be applicable, have preferred to suspend play while awaiting a ruling from officials summoned to the spot.

Now it is possible for a player in this situation to play the ball already in play, then adopt a different procedure with the second ball, and at the end of the round submit the facts for adjudication.

It has been necessary to hedge this rule with safeguards against abuse. The competitor must announce to his marker his intention to take advantage of this rule, and also state which ball he wants to score with if the rules permit. If for any reason the competitor fails to announce in advance his procedure or selection, the score with the second ball, if played in accordance with the rules, shall be his score for the hole.

A case of this kind occurred in the Dunlop-Masters tournament at Hollinwell. Eric Brown, the eventual winner, found his ball in a cutting behind the fifteenth green. If this were ditch or water hazard, Brown would have to either play the ball or pick it out and lose a stroke. Otherwise he could declare it unplayable. On the other hand, this might be a case for a "free drop." But to drop behind and then find that the cutting was neither a water hazard nor a casual obstacle coming under Rule 32 would involve him in a penalty of two strokes.

Brown therefore availed himself of Rule 11. He played the ball as it lay and holed out in six. Then he dropped a ball clear of the cutting and holed out in five. After official inspection the cutting was deemed to be "ground under repair," giving Brown a free drop, and his score with the second ball was accepted. Brown went on to win the tournament by three strokes, and it is a matter for conjecture whether he would have won if the hole had cost him six at a critical stage of the round.

But the incident shows how advantageous it must be to players to make themselves acquainted with the rules and their implications.

So far as the other sections of Rule 11 are concerned, several decisions have confirmed that claims must be made before any player in a match strikes from the next teeing-ground, or, in the case of the last hole of the round, before all the players have left the last green. This was so adjudged (Decision 54/12/27) in the case of a side taking an extra handicap stroke to which they were not entitled. As no claim had been made until the players returned to the clubhouse, the result had to stand.

And it was also ruled (Decision 56/103/44) that although a player who had holed out without being aware of the fact had actually holed his ball in fewer strokes than his opponent, he could not subsequently alter his acceptance of the opponent's claim that he had lost the hole by playing the wrong ball.

There are now six long rules (36 to 41) dealing mainly with the administration of competitions and the responsibility of competitors, and they bring together a large number of provisions once scattered through the rules. A hundred years ago the rules scarcely mentioned the organization of competitions except to stipulate that new holes be cut on Medal Day. But the Open Championship started in 1860 and by that time competitions were becoming more frequent. By the nineties there were special rules for medal-play which laid down the procedure for deciding ties and the marking and checking of score cards. In 1902 there were added special rules for match-play competitions (since discontinued) and the rules for three-ball, best-ball, and four-ball matches.

Right up to the experimental code of 1950 the special rules for stroke competitions remained, but when the present code was planned and the variations of rule for match- and medal-play were included under the same headings, it was deemed advisable to extract the rules of administration and incorporate them in separate rules at the end of the book. These define the duties and powers of the committee regarding arrangement of starting-time, decision of ties, defining the boundaries and practice areas, and making local rules. It should here be noted that, whereas before 1952 local committees were given a great deal of freedom in making local rules, they are now prohibited from making any rule which would waive a penalty applicable under the Rules of Golf.

There is the exception that if local conditions are held to interfere with the proper playing of the game and some variation of a Rule of Golf is necessary, the approval of the Governing Authority can be requested. Under this head would be permission to remove stones from bunkers in circumstances which would make them dangerous for players.

Another interesting point of Rule 36 is that, while the competition committee has no power to waive a Rule of Golf in dealing with an offence, the extreme penalty of disqualification can be modified in exceptional cases if the committee consider such action warranted. It has been ruled, however (Decision 53/39/60), that although a committee can arrange starting-times and the limits of the competition, it is not permitted to depart from such arrangements during the competition, except in exceptional circumstances. Other decisions have stressed the importance of committees providing for every eventuality in drawing up competition conditions. This is important in the decision of ties, alteration of handicaps during a running competition, and the application of handicap strokes in matches or ties extended beyond the original limits of the competition.

Failure by a competitor to sign his card (Decision 53/32/53) does not call for sympathetic treatment, and such a competitor is disqualified under Rule 36-5 if he has not signed within a reasonable time. Since the committee has the power to decide what is "reasonable time," the decision, nevertheless, must still be subject to local opinion. In this connection it may be pointed out that many golfers still seem to be ignorant of the fact that since 1950 it has been compulsory for the card to be signed by the competitor as well as by the marker.

There have been several decisions under Rule

37, mostly concerning the section penalizing players for suspending play on reaching the clubhouse at the end of nine holes or at some other part of the round. Between the wars any sheltering on the course or any discontinuance of play, even for bad weather, was punishable by disqualification, but now the competitor has a great deal of liberty, provided he does not delay play. He may stop if he thinks there is danger from lightning; return to the clubhouse to get waterproof clothing; or nip into the bar for a drink if held up by congestion on the tenth teeing-ground.

When two players are in a medal round it is convenient for each to mark the other's card, and in most matches the protagonists are left to settle their differences amicably if possible. But problems do occur in medal rounds for which neither side can find a solution; and needle matches sometimes find the players in uncompromising moods. In both cases points of law can be referred to the committee, but so that questions of fact can also be covered it is usual to appoint markers in important stroke competitions and referees and observers for important matches.

The term "referee" does not occur in the early rules, although even in the feather-ball days there were many big matches for heavy stakes which would have demanded the presence of some impartial official competent to decide controversial points.

By the middle of the nineteenth century the practice was well established, as we learn from the account of one of the great matches between Willie Park, Sr., and old Tom Morris. On that occasion, owing to the unfair tactics of the Musselburgh crowds who hampered Morris's play and interfered with the lie of his ball, Morris declined to continue the match and appealed to the referee, who stopped the match and directed that the stakes be drawn.

In those days the referee was no doubt content with seeing that each side had fair play and giving decisions on points of law, but it was not until 1902 that a referee's duties were officially defined: "An umpire or referee when appointed shall take cognisance of any breach of rule that he may observe, whether he be appealed to on the point or not." The present rule goes further (Definition 26): "A referee is appointed by the Committee to accompany the players to decide questions of fact and of golf law. He shall act on any breach of Rule or Local Rule which he may observe or which may be reported to him by an Observer. . . ."

The rules also make it clear that neither an observer nor a marker is a referee, and that none of these three officials is allowed to attend the flagstick, stand at or mark the position of the hole, or lift the ball or mark its position. It is important to note that the implication of Definition 26 is that a referee may not act on any breach of rule reported to him by anyone outside the match except a properly appointed observer.

The special rules for Bogey or Par competitions

(No. 39 in the present code) represent a comparatively new feature, and it is a curious fact that in the United States, where Colonel Bogey is now very much retired on half-pay, there were special rules of this kind some years before they existed in Britain, where the Colonel was born.

The U.S.G.A. had bogey rules in 1900 and the R. & A. did not follow suit until 1910. It would seem that the Bogey Competition, although a British invention, made bigger strides towards popularity in the United States than in Britain, probably because of the keenness of American golfers for playing against a standard. That the standard for them has become Old Man Par instead of Colonel Bogey has not affected their habits or attitude.

Colonel Bogey was born at Great Yarmouth in 1891, having been conceived the previous year in the mind of Mr. Hugh Rotherham, a member of the Coventry Golf Club. His idea was for playing against what he called the "ground score," or the score which a good golfer should take for a particular hole.

The first "ground score" competition took place in 1891 at Great Yarmouth, and the currency of the popular song "Hush, Hush, Hush, Here Comes the Bogey Man" led to the adoption of the name "Bogey." Later Bogey was introduced to the United Services Club at Portsmouth, where the members, finding him "a quiet, modest and retiring gentleman, uniformly steady but never over-brilliant," conferred on him the rank of Colonel.

This is not the way to climb to better things. Go out of the bunker the way you came in—and smooth your footmarks on the way out. (See Rule of Etiquette No. 6.)

To smooth the sand after playing a bunker shot is the act of a gentleman and a sportsman. After all, your neglect might be another's penalty—and you could be the innocent party next time. (See Rule of Etiquette No. 6.)

A pity, isn't it? So easy to replace the turf—so much more difficult for the greenkeeper to returf the place. So just put it back and tread it down, brother! (See Rule of Etiquette No. 7.)

The newly made officer went on a trip to the United States, where he was made very welcome. But since then the ideas and ambitions of Americans have soared beyond the narrow scope of Colonel Bogey, and he is no longer respected over there as a model of rectitude. Among Americans the term "Bogey" is used to signify a score one worse than the par for the hole, whereas on British courses the Standard Scratch Score (or par) is at most holes on the course synonymous with Bogey.

Even in Britain, however, Colonel Bogey does not occupy his previous proud and unchallenged position. A sprightly civilian named Stableford, after his progenitor, Dr. Frank Stableford of Wallasey, came on to the scene in 1932 and seems to have supplanted the Colonel in popular favour.

Unlike strict Colonel Bogey, who awards a "blob" to the player who cannot match or surpass his score, "Doctor" Stableford gives one point for a score one stroke worse than Bogey, two points for a "bogey," three points for a "birdie," and so on.

In the United States they have "Par Competitions," and our Stableford would be to them the equivalent of Bogey. Whether our standard of golf would be improved by substituting Par for Bogey as the Standard Scratch Score I cannot conjecture. My own view is that it is the state of mind which counts, not a form of words, and that our golfers will never be able to match the Americans in their ceaseless striving after perfection.

And since that striving makes itself evident by long, laborious rounds of fourball games with every putt holed out, every stroke noted, and nothing left to the imagination, I for one am not sorry. For us golf is still a game—and Colonel Bogey a nice old gentleman.

CHAPTER XV

Manners Makyth Golfers

ETIQUETTE is a code of behaviour, and one of the reasons for its inclusion in the rules is that golfers in the mass cannot or will not behave.

Everyone sooner or later offends against etiquette, mostly from forgetfulness but too frequently from a selfish indifference to the rights and convenience of others using the course.

A stranger to the game, reading these injunctions about moving or talking on the stroke, playing into the match ahead, holding up the course while searching for a ball, failing to replace divots and leaving bunkers unsmoothed, might be pardoned for imagining that the average golfer is an unprincipled hooligan who has not been "course-trained." We do not merit that description, but as a class we are inclined to get wrapped up in our own game and forget the existence of our fellow golfers. Most of us like to think we behave properly most of the time. Few of us could make unqualified claims to the halo of rectitude.

There are three main reasons for stressing the importance of etiquette—the great growth of the golfing population without a parallel increase in the number of courses; the tremendous improvement in course conditions during the past seventy years; and the advance in playing-technique and equipment.

To the second and third of these reasons paragraphs 6, 7, and 8 of "Etiquette" have a direct relation. When the "fair green" was a rough passage through the bushes and the iron club was used only for getting the ball out of hazards, there were no divots cut from turf. When practically everything on the course was a hazard except the "fair green" and the "hole green." And when there were no artificial bunkers and the natural ones were sandy depressions which were found as nature left them and left in the same state by any golfer unfortunate enough to be trapped in them. The "hole green" itself was also the teeing-ground and clubs were carried under the arm, so there was no occasion for concern about players or caddies standing close to the hole, dropping bags on the green, or carelessly replacing the flagstick. Nowadays, with smooth greens, neatly cut holes, kempt fairways, and raked bunkers, the acts of careless, ignorant, or selfish golfers are at once apparent.

The player who cuts a divot and neglects to replace it not only makes a scar which will cost time and money to heal, but also creates a difficulty for any following player unlucky enough to find his ball in the divot mark. In the same way, failure to remove traces of a visit to a bunker, or to repair pitch marks on the putting-green, makes work for the staff and possible trouble for fellow players.

Adherence to other provisions of etiquette depends on the character of the golfer and what attempts can be made to bring up young players in the way they should go, and bring home to adults the desirability of co-operation.

The first reference to etiquette in the rules consists of the following preliminary paragraph to the code of 1888: "It is the duty of every golfer to replace or see replaced any portions of turf which may have been cut out by the act of playing." In 1899 the rules of etiquette, largely as they read today, were included as a supplement to the rules, and in 1919 they were given greater force by being printed between the general rules and those for match-play competitions.

For the next fifty years "Etiquette" followed the rules and was distinct from them, but in 1949, although still distinct, it was printed before the rules. Mr. Bernard Darwin, at that time chairman of the Rules of Golf Committee, stated that this had been done "to emphasize the duty of players to familiarize themselves with the long-established customs and usages of the Game."

Two years later the joint Anglo-American committee incorporated "Etiquette" in the rules by making it Section 1 under the general heading "The Rules of Golf." But this step, although streamlining the code and emphasizing the official view that golfers ought to be encouraged to regard the rules of etiquette as of equal importance with the rules of the game, does not give etiquette the power of rules. No penalty is laid down for any breach, except indirectly by the fact that if a golfer holds up following players by looking for a ball or playing slowly he is delaying play and therefore liable to be penalized under Rule 37.

But there is no penalty for moving or talking on the shot, standing close to the ball while another player is addressing it, or for not complying with the injunction about replacing divots and repairing bunkers. So far as the first point is concerned, it is obviously impossible for the rules to legislate against gamesmanship—public opinion must take care of that. And, however much we might like to have some kind of rule to punish those who damage the course and create difficulties for following players, life would become intolerable, and matches and competitions decidedly acrimonious, if faults of that kind were made the subject of claims by players or action by referees.

The big snag about real rules of etiquette with appropriate penalties is that such rules could apply in practice only to tournaments and competitions and not to friendly games in which such breaches most often occur.

So this chapter ends as it began with the problem unsolved. Etiquette is a code of behaviour, and only by education can we hope to achieve general observation of its precepts.

CHAPTER XVI

Amateurism—and After

ONE of the results of the blurred moral values of today is the extreme difficulty of deciding who is and who is not an amateur sportsman.

The literal meaning—a lover of the game for the game's sake—has lost most of its original significance owing to changed circumstances and the taint of commercialism. Golf is not perhaps so affected by this trend as some other sports, but it is true to say that among low-handicap golfers, while many are genuine admitted professionals earning their living at the game, a great number are "amateurs" who get more out of golf than merely the pleasure of playing it.

Sorting the sheep from the goats is a complex problem, and when we find a complete section of the rules, consisting of four rules, twenty-seven para-

graphs, and more than one thousand words, devoted
to it we might well ask whether defining the border-
line is worth all that trouble. If this elaborate set of
regulations is necessary to preserve the purity of the
amateur status—and, in the opinion of many, fails to
do so—is it not time the amateur status was
abandoned in favour of something more in keeping
with the times?

A century ago there was no need for rules of
amateurism. An amateur played the game for fun
at his own expense and a professional was paid for
doing it. The amateur sometimes won money by
wagering on his skill, and the professional sometimes
had to play merely for fun, but that did not alter
or weaken the distinction between the two classes.
There was a clear line of demarcation and no one
had anything to hide.

Then commercialism crept in. Golf became an
industry as well as a game. The newspapers took
interest in it, people wrote books about it, and finally
came the publicity of radio and television. And one
may well ask now: when does amateurism stop and
non-amateurism begin?

It is difficult to distinguish between the representative of a golf-ball firm who wins a championship
and the championship winner who gets a job with a
golf-ball firm; between the golf writer who becomes
an international and the international who takes to
writing golf. And who is to say whether the promis-
ing young amateur who gets a post in the office of a

golf-keen stockbroker is preferred for his promise at golf or his potentialities as a financier?

There must be many cases in which the verdict could go either way. And the amateur laws have many loopholes. Take the question of caddies. Before he is twenty-one a youngster can carry clubs for hire without forfeiting his amateur status. If over twenty-one he loses his amateur status if he receives compensation for "carrying regularly as a caddie." And "regularly" is defined as "carrying golf clubs as his main or substantial source of income."

This allows a man who works five days a week as a casual labourer and carries clubs every week-end to play in amateur competitions. How on earth can anyone investigating such a case determine whether the casual labour of the week-end caddying represents the "main or substantial income"?

More publicity was given in 1957 to the action of the United States Golf Association in putting on a year's probation the reigning U.S. amateur champion because certain expenses incurred in playing in championships had been paid by his employer. For every case like that there must be thousands involving less well-known players, and I think the time has come for a new approach by both Great Britain and the United States to a problem which is likely to grow more acute.

With that suggestion I end this review of the Rules of Golf—a review which I hope has given some idea of the development of the rules, some conception of their purpose, and some guide as to how they have been and should be applied.

Now it remains to look at the future and see what the rules are likely to become. Because no one, with the history of the last two hundred years in mind, can believe in the immutability of the present code. The old rules were destined not to endure "in all time coming," and the present rules must change —if not in this decade, then in the next. And all thinking golfers ought to ask themselves the questions: How must they change? What in fact do we want in the Rules of Golf?

It was not part of my assignment to offer any concrete proposals for altering the rules, nor is it my intention to do so. Apart from the very presumption of the idea that an individual could even begin to throw down or substantially remodel an edifice erected with such care on such deep foundations, any large-scale revision, even if it were considered necessary, could be undertaken only by a body of international golf jurists having a mandate from the world of golf.

But these considerations do not prevent me from making some observations on the rules generally and their effect on the future of the game, because, while this book has been written as a work of history and a work of reference, it has several subsidiary objects. One of these is the stimulation of rules-consciousness among ordinary golfers, the men and women—and juniors—who, far from the glamour, the bustle, and the stress of championship and tournament golf, play their week-end games in a state of bliss induced, if not by ignorance, at least by an imperfect knowledge of the language and the meaning of the rules.

Since the game of golf is subject to many more varieties of incident than any other game, the code controlling it must necessarily be voluminous and subject to alteration or embellishment from time to time in the light of practical experience. As I have shown, the many revisions of the rules have ranged in the last two centuries from minor modifications to wholesale overhauls. And it would be foolish to assume the process of change is complete.

Our ancestors, reading their thirteen rules scribbled on a sheet of foolscap, regarded them complacently as certain to endure. But the history of the next two hundred years showed how impossible it is for one body of men, however sincere and however knowledgeable, to evolve a set of rules providing for every contingency and pleasing everyone.

While conscious of this, and content to allow the ordinary processes of change and pressure of public opinion to influence our rule-makers for the common good, I am convinced that neither the rules in their present form nor the Rules of Golf Committee in their present state of Olympian aloofness have the power to educate the popular mind.

The rules themselves—something like twenty-five thousand words—are sufficiently long and detailed to deter anyone save the enthusiast from attempting to study them. Probably not more than a minority of the golf population of Great Britain have even looked inside the books except to glance at the rules when first issued and to investigate individual cases or settle clubhouse arguments. For this reason, while most golfers, if they take the trouble, can find the answers to most of their problems, few are capable of avoiding the commission of illegal acts or knowing when such acts are committed by others.

If a golfer does not know his rights under the rules, he has only himself to blame, but in his torts he is affecting the play of others, and evasion of the rules, even unintentionally, may have far-reaching consequences. It is particularly important that a golfer should know the rules when playing in a stroke competition, for his unconscious condonation of faults in his fellow competitor is a betrayal of the rights of all the other competitors.

So the lay-out of the rule-book should include a summary of Do's and Don't's which could be memorized or at least referred to by the golfer in case of trouble. For example:

BUNKER—In a bunker you may not
      Ground your club.
      Remove any loose impediment.
PUTTING-GREEN—On the putting-green when it is not your turn to play you may not

Attend the flagstick or lift your ball unless requested to do so by opponent or fellow competitor.

It may be argued that the provision of a quick guide of this kind would tend to deter people from studying the complete rules. I take the opposite view. It is much more likely to encourage them to learn more about the rules.

The complexities of our motoring laws, for example, are beyond the comprehension of most motorists, who look at the Road Acts, if they ever do look at them, only when in trouble for some alleged offence. But the Government has provided motorists with a guide to behaviour and conduct on the roads, and it is an implied condition of holding a driving-licence that one has studied the Highway Code.

For similar reasons I think golfers should have a Course Code which would be supplementary to, but not a substitute for, the Rules of Golf.

As for the Olympian aloofness of the Rules of Golf Committee, I mean nothing derogatory by that description. The members of this Committee do a great deal of work voluntarily in their spare time and deal not only with frivolous or unnecessary questions (which they answer with great patience) but also with problems of the greatest importance.

All golfers should be grateful for their efforts, but I submit with respect that their services should not end with the formulation of rules and the production of case law. I hope to see the day when the Rules of Golf Committee will dictate policy and start a campaign for spreading knowledge of the rules among ordinary golfers.

It is important, for example, that youngsters should grow up with the idea that knowledge of the rules is part of the game. Much good work of that kind is being done at many clubs, but it lacks a central directive. There have also been isolated attempts at the education of adult golfers by rules quizzes, films, and other devices, but many of those activities would have carried more weight and reached a larger circle if there had been a campaign directed by St. Andrews or the four National Unions.

The United States Golf Association, in addition to holding the balance neatly between progressive development of the rules and conservative adherence to tradition, has in recent years made tremendous strides in this matter of mass education. The insistence on rules and rule-keeping is inherent in the activities of the U.S.G.A. and since the war two films, one about the rules and the other about etiquette, have been produced officially for use by golf clubs and other interested communities. So far as I know, only one such film has been produced in this country, and that not by a governing body.

Many U.S.G.A. officials have from time to time made forthright pronouncements on the need for rules education, and typical of these efforts is the following extract from an article in the *U.S.G.A.*

Journal by Ralph W. Miller, a member of the Junior Championship Committee:

Golfers who think the rules too strict and complicated should play a match under the early rules which were very few and simple. They would soon become satisfied and even happy with the present ones.

It is safe to say the average golfer has never read the rules. The only thing he knows about them is what was told to him by someone who likewise never read them. The time he devotes to golf is spent in trying to improve his swing.

Golf, of course, is a game of skill. However, there are many things in golf other than the ability to hit the ball.

You have many rights and privileges which, if you know them, and occasion arises to exercise them, will affect your play and score and possibly determine the outcome of a competition. Such things are not found in a smooth swing; they are in the rule-book.

Much more, I am sure, could be done with the help of films in Great Britain. After all, television has taken golf into the homes of millions of people who have scarcely ever heard of the game. Some of those millions are going to be added to the golf population. Many of them will have neither the intelligence nor the educational background and training to assimilate twenty-five thousand words of rules or have a clear understanding of the moral issues involved and how they are affected by tradition.

The rules do not allow the repair of pitchmarks before putting—but Etiquette demands that this be done afterwards. (See Rule of Etiquette No. 7.)

Damage to greens by golf balls cannot be prevented, but this kind of damage is inexcusable. Bags dropped on the green so that club-heads press into the turf, flagsticks carelessly thrown down, making toemarks in turf, and using putter shafts as props—all these involuntary and thoughtless actions mean trouble for the next player and more work for the greenkeeper.

It is for this great new population, as well as for those who have long been adherents of the Royal and Ancient Game, that an effort at government level is necessary—an effort to make us more rules-conscious as a nation, and thereby adding to the pleasure which this grand pastime can give.

The rules, as I have tried to show, have their roots in tradition, but are now operated in a great democracy of golf in which plain speaking and plain dealing are alike essential. They are there to be used and observed, and all that golfers and golf governments can do should be done to ensure that the rules are not just a collection of regulations in a closed book, but a living code followed and honoured by every man, woman, and child playing on the links.

Index

i

Index

Index

A NOTE ON THE AUTHOR

GEOFFREY ESMOND COUSINS was born in
London on November 26, 1900. From 1919
to 1933 he was chief reporter of the Golf
News Agency, London. For the succeeding
six years he served as golf correspondent
for the Press Association, of which he was
foreign editor from 1939 to 1945. Since 1938
he has been Honourable Secretary of the
Association of Golf Writers of Great Britain,
which he helped to found, and since 1945
he has been golf correspondent of the *Star*
(London), in which his "At the 19th Hole,"
one of the most widely read columns in all
golf journalism, appears weekly. Mr. Cousins wrote the script for the Spalding film
Golf to Rule. He contributes widely to
periodicals, including *Golf Monthly,* in
which his writings appear regularly.

A NOTE ON THE TYPE AND PRODUCTION

The text of this book is set in Caledonia, a Linotype face designed by W. A. Dwiggins (1880–1956), who was responsible for so much that is good in contemporary book design. Though much of his early work was in advertising and he was the author of the standard volume Layout in Advertising, Mr. Dwiggins later devoted his prolific talents to book typography and type design, and worked with great distinction in both fields. In addition to his designs for Caledonia, he created the Metro, Electra, and Eldorado series of type faces, as well as a number of experimental cuttings that have never been issued commercially.

Caledonia belongs to the family of printing types called "modern face" by printers—a term used to mark the change in style of typeletters that occurred at the end of the eighteenth century. It is best evidenced in the letter shapes designed by Baskerville, Martin, Bodoni, and the Didots.

This book was composed, printed, and bound by H. Wolff, New York. The paper was manufactured by S. D. Warren Company, Boston.